Transport Economic Theory

Transport Economic Theory

Sergio Jara-Díaz

Universidad de Chile
Santiago, Chile

ELSEVIER

Amsterdam – Boston – Heidelberg – London – New York – Oxford – Paris
San Diego – San Francisco – Singapore – Sydney – Tokyo

Elsevier
Linacre House, Jordan Hill, Oxford OX2 8DP, UK
Radarweg 29, PO Box 211, 1000 AE Amsterdam, The Netherlands

First edition 2007

British Library Cataloguing in Publication Data
A catalogue record for this book is available from the British Library

Library of Congress Cataloging-in-Publication Data
A catalog record for this book is available from the Library of Congress

ISBN: 978-0-08-045028-5

For information on all Elsevier publications
visit our website at books.elsevier.com

Printed and bound in The Netherlands

07 08 09 10 11   10 9 8 7 6 5 4 3 2 1

Working together to grow
libraries in developing countries

www.elsevier.com | www.bookaid.org | www.sabre.org

ELSEVIER   BOOK AID International   Sabre Foundation

To my family
To my students

About the Author

Sergio Jara-Díaz is Professor at the Transport Systems Division of the University of Chile in Santiago, a research unit he helped to found in the early seventies that became a forerunner in establishing transport as a distinctive field of knowledge in that country. He obtained his Ph.D. from the Massachusetts Institute of Technology (MIT) in 1981 with a thesis in the field of Transport Economics. He has published more than seventy research articles in books and journals focusing on users' behaviour and benefits, value of time, scale and scope economies in transport network industries, public transport and pricing. Professor Jara-Díaz has designed and taught courses in Transport Economics both at the University of Chile and MIT, and teaches regularly in many universities in Spain. He has been a member of the Highest Commission of Academic Evaluation at the University of Chile; is a member of the American Economic Association, the Association for European Transport, and a founding member of the Chilean Society of Transport Engineering. He has been running a weekly radio show since 1991 and has published a book of chronicles and short stories.

Prologue

This book is an attempt at settling a debt I have with my students - past and present - and with myself. I have been doing research in transport economics since the seventies and I delivered my first formal basic course in the area in 1982, whose contents have evolved slowly but continuously without changing the structure. From the very beginning I was guided by the conviction that this was not a matter of teaching microeconomics with an application to transport; introducing time and space was unavoidable and that made a significant difference. This posed a challenge that translated into systematic work devoted to construct the basic aspects that I thought constituted the foundations of a body of knowledge that could be properly called Transport Economic Theory.

I remember vividly the day when, twenty eight years ago as a student at MIT, the late Ann Friedlander gave me a pile of papers dealing with the theory of multiple products, asking me to read them and write a short essay on how I would apply this to transport. Matching what I read with my view of transport as a "flows production" activity was instantaneous. In essence, my answer was that this new theory was really the only way to properly understand transport production, as any transport firm produces a vector of origin-destination flows and, therefore, concepts like economies of scope would help the analysis of network growth and shape in transport industries. My dear Professor, whose recent contribution had been the hedonic treatment of transport output, told me that although she could not see exactly what I meant, I had a Ph.D. thesis there. The chapter on transport production is the long run result of a research line that begun that day. I still have that handwritten essay.

Many individuals have contributed to my enjoyment with Transport Economics. Tristán Gálvez introduced me to the world of flows in the early seventies when I was a student at the University of Chile. By the end of the decade I was exposed to the microeconomics of discrete choices in a course taught by Dan McFadden at MIT; I loved the simplicity of the idea that allowed the introduction of quality with only a slight extension of consumer's behavior theory. Later on this was the pillar on which I was able to develop a better understanding of the role of personal income and propose new measures of users' benefits. My work on the microeconomics of demand received the permanent support of my friend and colleague Juan de Dios Ortúzar, from the Catholic University of Chile, whose faith applying my theories has played an important role in this story. Similar appreciation has always been explicitly shown by David Hensher from the University of Sydney in his many books and papers, by Huw Williams from Cardiff University, and by Ken Small from the University of California, Irvine.

Many dear colleagues around the world, perhaps too many to mention, have contributed in different ways with their time and care to keep academic interaction alive and pleasurable. I want to explicitly acknowledge Hani Mahmassani, formerly at U. of Texas at Austin and now at the U. of Maryland, Yossi Sheffi and Nigel Wilson from MIT, Peter Mackie from the U. of Leeds, Pablo Coto-Millán from the U. of Cantabria, Eduardo Martínez-Budría from U. of La Laguna and José Holguín-Veras from RPI. My colleagues at the Transport Division of the University of Chile were always supportive of the work behind the book, and I do thank Francisco Martínez, Marcela Munizaga, Cristián Cortés and Leonardo Basso for their daily life patience.

The final stages of the preparation of this book received the very important editorial help of former student Rodrigo Quijada with the assistance of present student Alejandro Tirachini. Rodrigo offered his help and took his duties as if this book was his; from discussions with him the structure, wording and general presentation of the chapters improved indeed.

Neither research along these years nor this book have stolen time from my family, as nothing could have deprived me from the pleasures of making my children sleep, of playing, singing, studying and talking with them along their lives. This, of course, was induced by my own education with my parents Sergio and Elena. My sons Pedro (Santiago, 1977) and Francisco (Boston, 1980), and these many years with the woman I love, Momy, are the meaning of life to me. They have always been first priority.

Sergio Jara-Díaz
Santiago, January 2007.

Table of Contents

Presentation

The study of Transport is the study of movement, of displacements of individuals and things in both space and time. But unlike the displacement of, for example, water particles in a piping system, the distinctive feature of Transport as an area of knowledge is the involvement of human *will* in the process. On one hand, our "particles" have will; each one needs to go from some point to some other point in space-time, and this makes them no-interchangeable. On the other hand, some elements of our "piping system" have will as well; they decide how many particles can go together, how frequently they can travel, or how fast they move. Those that are responsible for the particles' will, be it passengers or freight, are the **users** of the transportation system, and those responsible for the moving elements of the piping system are the **operators**.

Will means tastes, preferences, decision-making, objective pursuing, perceptions, rationality; all together. It means *behavior*. So in principle, if we are interested in analyzing the behavior of either transport users or operators, we can rely upon fairly well established theories of economic behavior. On the users' side, individual demand for trips could be studied with the concepts of consumer theory, and freight demand could be looked at as part of firms' decisions, either to bring inputs to the plant or to distribute output to markets, such that transport is an input to the complete production process. On the other side, the behavior of transport operators can be in most cases understood using the tools of the theory of the firm, although in this case the product is the vector of displacements itself. But despite being useful as forms to approach the problem, basic production and consumption theories do not explicitly account for the key dimensions in transportation processes: **time and space**. In fact, introducing them is nearly what it is all about to formulate a transport economic theory. And this is exactly the intention behind this book.

Let us briefly point out some of the key issues that **have** to be included in a framework to understand and analyze transportation activities. First, for the operator to be able to produce movements, what is being moved has to be physically present; this is common to nearly all services and makes an obvious difference with respect to the production of goods in general, which does not require the consumer' presence. This has been sometimes referred to as the "non-storability" property of transportation processes. Second, this same fact can be looked at from the users' viewpoint, which means that own time is needed to actually realize the product; again, this is common to all kinds of consumption, but here it is usually the single most important dimension of the "product". Thirdly, as each complete displacement in space-time is a different product, transportation firms usually generate a vector of products as opposed to a single (scalar) output; thus, the supply side of transportation services should be looked at as multioutput processes. Although it is true that most productive activities involve more than one product, here this characteristic is unavoidable when going into minimally relevant economic analysis. Movements in different directions are different products, and simple descriptions like ton-kilometers only hide what is part of the essence of transportatio n analysis: origins, destinations, networks.

Therefore, many characteristics make the economic analysis of transport systems operation very different from a straight application of the concepts contained in microeconomic textbooks. As explained, most (if not all) of these characteristics are not exclusive to the analysis of movements, but their simultaneous presence (plus others not mentioned here) make transport economics a somewhat specialized field as opposed to an area of application. And this is so accounting only for technical-analytical considerations, not yet including the social and/or political dimensions usually involved.

The book is organized around four central topics: the transport firm itself; individual's decision-making regarding travel; accounting users' benefits from changes in the transport market; and optimal pricing, encompassing all the previous elements; a chapter has been devoted to each one of them. In Chapter 1, Transport Production, the basic theory of the firm is extended to account for time and space explicitly, showing the multiproduct nature of the transport firm. It is discussed how operator's decisions about route structure, frequency, points served and so on, plus their relation with network characteristics, determine input requirements to produce a desired output; simple cyclical systems help illustrating the concepts. Next, a basic supply-oriented microeconomic tool is introduced: the cost function. Its evident multioutput nature is used to understand rigorously the meaning of scale, scope and complementarity in transportation operations. Building on this, traditional analysis like determining marginal costs or degree of scale economies –which are typically used to study the convenience of expanding production- are looked at here paying attention to the spatial dimension of transport production, unveiling along the way some mistakes that are still common in the analysis of transport cost structures and industry organization.

In Chapter 2, Travel Demand and Value of Time, individuals' behavior is explored starting from the traditional utility-maximization approach, but considering discrete-choice formulations that are able to handle the type of decisions people have to make when facing alternative modes of transport. Needless to say, the amount of time needed to be spent by using an alternative appears as a fundamental variable, just as important –or even more-than price is in traditional consumer modeling. All services require consumers to put in their time in order to provide the service in question, but in the case of transport time is undoubtedly at the center of the issue. Not only that, unlike time spent in a restaurant or at the movies, time spent in mandatory transport is normally undesired and even unpleasant, so people would gladly pay for reducing it as much as possible. As a consequence, this willingness-to-pay-to-reduce-travel-time, or more broadly, individuals' valuation of their own time, is a key element in the transport field. However and despite its obvious importance, it is surprising to realize how slow the progress has been regarding our understanding of the way people manage their time in general. The role and evolution of time as a variable in consumer theory is discussed in this Chapter, which finishes with the presentation of a more complete model encompassing leisure, work, travel, and their values.

Valuation of Users' Benefits in Transport Systems constitutes Chapter 3, and there, as the name suggests, different measures to estimate users' benefits arising from changes in the transport system –like those a new transport project would make- are presented and discussed. The simple and most widely used measures are shown and their limitations exposed, followed by less popular but rigorous measures derived directly, as opposed to the former, from the general microeconomic theory. The chapter also covers two other related topics. First, an analysis is made about the link between benefits measures directly in the transport market and those one could measure in the markets that generated the transport demand in the first place. This means examining, for example, benefits from commercial activities produced by people who traveled for shopping. Second, the issue of aggregating benefits from different users for matters of determining benefits at a society level is discussed. This means, stated in more practical terms, analyzing the difference between transport projects that are financed by users directly and those undertaken with tax money.

In the final chapter, Optimal Transport Pricing, a look is taken at different pricing strategies and their consequences. It starts presenting the desired case where price reflects economic efficiency, which helps illustrating that neither private transport nor public transport markets would produce such case if left alone, due to the presence of externalities. The necessary correction -from a regulatory point of view- that needs to be implemented for each case in order to reach efficiency is also presented. Next, alternative forms of pricing aiming at different goals other than economic efficiency are analyzed.

Transport industries are certainly among the most interesting as a subject of study. The inherent spatial characteristic of this activity and its repercussions for firm cost structure analysis, the presence of externalities of significant magnitude, the fact that users do not want this product by itself but only as a mean to solve some other need, the unavoidable restriction faced by all individuals of having to organize their activities, travel among them, within a 24-hour time frame, and the rather public nature of this market, which forces national and regional authorities to design, evaluate and finance transport projects with social welfare in mind, make this field of knowledge a very special and challenging one. This book aims at providing a theoretical ground for its understanding.

1.   Transport production and cost structure

1.1.   Introduction

As transport activities mean movement of individuals and goods in both time and space, the analysis of transport productio n involves the assignment of resources to generate trips between several different points in space during various periods. As a conse quence, the microeconomic analysis of transport production is far from a simple extension of the traditional theory of the firm. In this chapter we present the underpinnings of a microeconomic theory of the transport firm, with particular emphasis on the nature of the technical relations between inputs and outputs (production or transformation function) and the use of the cost function as a tool to obtain valuable information for the design of transport policies as pricing and regulation.

The chapter begins with the notion of transport production, including the definition of transport output, the role of space, the idea of operating rules, and the concept of scale, all of which are illustrated using simple cyclical systems. Then the cost function and its properties regarding the calculation of marginal costs, economies of scale and economies of scope, are presented and explained within the context of transport systems analysis. A synthesis of the empirical work using transport cost functions is then offered, with special emphasis on the adequate treatment of output in its specification, and on the difficulties with the prevailing approach to analyze industry structure. Improved procedures to calculate scale and spatial scope economies correctly when output aggregates are used are included, plus a discussion about the analysis of the industry structure considering such measures.

1.2.   Transport production

1.2.1.   Product and technology

Basically, the production of goods and services can be synthetically described using the concepts of inputs, outputs and technology. Inputs have to be acquired by the firm in order to be combined - within the boundaries of process-specific rules – so as to produce outputs. For a given level of outputs, the firm has to choose type and amount of inputs, as well as a subset of combination rules. Technology defines all feasible input combinations. Formally, let X be the inputs vector (quantity/time unit) and Y the outputs vector. Then,

Definition 1.1: Technology
The technology T is defin ed by all $(X,Y) \in T \Leftrightarrow Y$ can be produced from X.

A transport process is the immediate effect of the action of transporting, i.e., moving some physical entity from a certain origin in space-time to a certain destination in space-time. We can associate this concept with that of "product" in an economic sense, with some reservations. To describe a product we refer to its qualitative characteristics, assigning a name for simplicity (e.g., oranges, shoes, etc.). To measure a product we need a physical unit of reference, and a quantity in terms of these physical units (e.g., 5 tons of oranges, or

1000 pairs of shoes). When we talk about a production process we need flow units, as opposed to stock units (e. g., 1000 pairs of shoes per week).

But to measure a transport process we would need: a qualitative description of what is being transported, a physical unit of reference, quantity (flow) in terms of these units, and origin and destination in space-time. **The need to explicitly establish origin and destination in space-time is the characteristic that distinguishes more clearly a transport product from the traditional concept**. The transport firm has to use vehicles, terminals, rights-of-way, energy, labor, and so on, to produce movements - freight and/or passengers - from several origins to several destinations during different periods. Thus, **the output of a transport process is a *vector*,**

$$Y = \left\{ y_{ij}^{kt} \right\} \in R^{KxNxT}$$ (1.1)

where each component y_{ij}^{kt} represents the flow of type k moved from origin i to destination j (O-D pair ij) within period t, for example passengers from Paris to Frankfurt during a specific weekend (K, N and T are the number of flow types, the number of O-D pairs, and the number of time periods, respectively).

Expression (1.1) is fairly general, including the possibility of a transport firm dealing with several flow types (persons, goods of different types), but it is quite important to stress that **a transport firm produces multiple products mainly because of the presence of time and *space* (periods and origin-destination pairs), not by the handling of multiple flow types**. The word "product" is used in this chapter to indicate a given flow type in a given period between a given O-D pair. Even if a firm only offers passenger service, it still will be offering multiple products. Moving passengers from New York to Buenos Aires for Christmas will usually involve different inputs combinations than doing it from Tokyo to Moscow in June; they are indeed two different products. Unlike the classical theory of the firm, a transport company participates in several markets simultaneously, each with its own demand curve and its own marginal costs, although the latter are usually interrelated. And note the spatial dimension –much more importantly than time- is the key aspect distinguishing the transport industry from other economic activities.

Now, for a given set of flows in Y, the firm has to make several choices: number and capacity of vehicles (fleet size), design of the rights-of-way (location, flow capacity), design of terminals (location, loading-unloading capacity), vehicle frequencies, and so on. Some of these decisions involve choosing the characteristics of inputs, and some are related with their use, i.e. with the form in which inputs are combined to accommodate the flow vector. We will call these latter types of choices **operating rules**. Because transport production takes place on a network, a transport firm has to decide, as well, **a service structure** –i.e. the generic way in which vehicles will visit the nodes to produce the flows– and a **link sequence**. These two endogenous decisions define a **route structure**, which has to be chosen using exogenous spatial information, namely the **O-D structure** of demand (defined by the vector Y), the **location of the nodes** and the **physical network**. Note that the need to make a decision on a route structure is, in the end, a consequence of the spatial dimension of product.

For a given type of transport firm (for example interurban buses) some of the decisions related with the acquisition of inputs are constrained, because of the existence of common infrastructure (for example the road system) or the rigidity of input markets (for example fleet size). On the other hand, decisions on operating rules are generally made within the boundaries of existing inputs.

Example 1.1

Consider an O-D system with three nodes, a single period and a single flow type, as in Figure 1.1.a, located on a physical network, as in Figure 1.1.b. For a given set of flows $\{v_{ij}\}$, the appropriate combination of inputs and operating rules would depend on many factors. Three possible service structures are shown in Figure 1.2 (Jara-Díaz, 2000). Structure (a) corresponds to a general cyclical system (Gálvez, 1978), structure (b) corresponds to three simple cyclical systems (direct service) and structure (c), where a distribution node is created, is known as *hub-and-spoke* and is very common in air transport (note that *hub* H may or may not coincide with an origin or destination node). Regarding vehicle assignment to fleets, which is part of the service structure, there is no choice but one fleet (one frequency) in case (a), three fleets in case (b) and one, two (with three alternatives) or three fleets in case (c). If a cyclical counter-clockwise system like the one in Figure 1.2.a was chosen, a possible route structure could be the one shown in Figure 1.3.

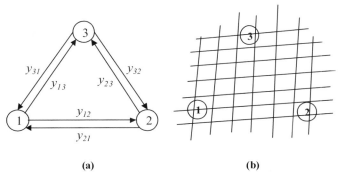

(a)   (b)

Figure 1.1. *O-D structure and physical network*

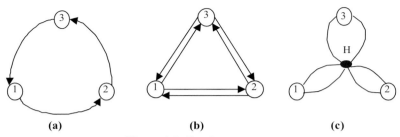

(a)   **(b)**   **(c)**

Figure 1.2. *Service structures*

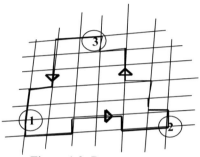

Figure 1.3. *Route structure*

Both service and route structures should be analyzed in parallel with vehicle size and frequency in order to make the most convenient choice. If this was either a road or a railway system, the physical structure of the road network would constrain the choice of routes and schedules. Moreover, for a given fleet size (including vehicle capacity), scheduling would be the only decision to make.

The technical relation between inputs and outputs is summarized through the concept of a transformation or production function. Concisely,

Definition 1.2: Transformation function
$F(X,Y)$ represents the transformation function if $(X,Y) \in T \Leftrightarrow F(X,Y) \geq 0$. Equality represents technical optimality (efficiency).

1.2.2. The simple cyclical system

Let us apply these concepts using the simplest possible case, the two nodes system. Consider a single O-D pair, single product, single period (Gálvez, 1978; Jara-Díaz, 1982b) and let *Y* be the flow from O to D. Define

B = fleet size
K = capacity per vehicle
k = load size per vehicle
$t(k)$ = travel time *en route* as a function of load size
μ = loading & unloading speed

Then Y/k vehicles per unit time are needed to satisfy demand and each vehicle takes $t_c = t(k) + 2(k/\mu) + t(0)$ units of time to complete a cycle (loading, moving, unloading and returning). Then Y/k equals B/t_c is equivalent to

$$Y \equiv \frac{Bk}{t(k) + 2\dfrac{k}{\mu} + t(0)} \qquad (1.2)$$

For a given B and μ, one can find the value of k that maximizes Y, k^*. It can be easily proved that k^* would be given by vehicle capacity K, provided the effect of k on travel time is small. Therefore,

$$Y \leq \frac{BK}{t(K) + 2\dfrac{K}{\mu} + t(0)} = h(B, K, \mu) \qquad (1.3)$$

where $h(B, K, \mu)$ is the production function which gives the maximum flow for a given set of inputs B, K and μ. Note that in this case the transformation function is $F(B, K, \mu, Y) = h(B, K, \mu) - Y$. The optimal combination of inputs for a given value of Y, would depend on the relative prices of vehicles and loading-unloading capacity. In this simple cyclical system, the input choice, their feasible combinations and the operating rule can be clearly distinguished.

Thus, depending on the characteristics of the particular transport system, the transport firm could adjust inputs and operating rules according to the different levels of Y. This concept remains when Y is a vector. The simplest possible version of a multioutput transport firm is one serving a backhaul system with two nodes (1 and 2) and two flows (y_{12} and y_{21}) of a single product during a single period (Gálvez, 1978; Jara-Díaz, 1982b): Let us assume for simplicity that the firm operates the same fleet to move both flows. Then vehicle frequency in both directions is the same and given by the maximum necessary, which in turn depends upon the relative flows; let us assume $y_{12} \geq y_{21}$. Then the technical optimum requires the vehicles in the $1 \rightarrow 2$ direction to be fully loaded, and frequency will be given by

$$f = \frac{y_{12}}{K} \tag{1.4}$$

The load size in the opposite direction, k_{21}, will be

$$k_{21} = \frac{y_{21}}{f} = \frac{y_{21}}{y_{12}} K \tag{1.5}$$

The fleet size needed, B, has to be equal to f times cycle time t_c which, under our simplifying assumption, is given by

$$t_c = t_{12}(K) + \frac{2K}{\mu} + \frac{2}{\mu} \frac{y_{21}}{y_{12}} K + t_{21}(k_{21}) \tag{1.6}$$

Just for the sake of simplicity, let us see the case characterized by vehicle speed v independent of load size and potentially different route distances d_{ij} in each direction. Then, using equations (1.4) and (1.6), the equality $B = f t_c$ turns into

$$BK = y_{12}\left[\frac{d_{12}}{v} + 2\frac{K}{\mu} + \frac{d_{21}}{v}\right] + 2\frac{K}{\mu} y_{21} \tag{1.7}$$

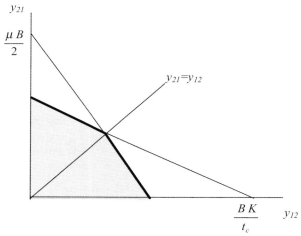

Figure 1.4. *Production possibility frontier of the backhaul system.*

As this is valid for $y_{12} \geq y_{21}$, and there is a symmetric expression for $y_{21} \geq y_{12}$, the general result for the technical relation among flows and inputs is

$$y_{ij} = \frac{\mu B}{2} - \left(\frac{(d_{12} + d_{21})\mu}{2Kv} + 1\right) y_{ji}, \forall y_{ji} \geq y_{ij} \tag{1.8}$$

Noting that the slope of $y_{ij} = h(y_{ji})$ is negative and less than -1, it is fairly simple to show that the graphical representation of the backhaul system in the output space looks like Figure 1.4. Equation (1.8) represents the production or transformation function of the system, and the shaded area in the figure represents all the vectors (y_{12}, y_{21}) that can be produced with a given fleet B, and capacities μ and K, but only the boundary represents optimal usage. This boundary is the production possibility frontier, whose symmetry is derived from the assumption of load independence of speed.

1.2.3. The three nodes system

Let us consider now the three nodes system with a six flows O-D structure (see Figure 1.1.a), with nodes connected by three links of length d_{ij} (Jara-Díaz and Basso, 2003). Note that for this simple physical network, the choice of a service structure is conveniently coincidental with the choice of a route structure because there is no decision on link sequence. We will keep the simplifying assumptions of the previous example, namely the sequential loading/unloading procedure and known values of K, μ and v. Let us begin with a general cyclical counter-clockwise structure (Figure 1.2.a), which implies the use of one fleet only. In this case, vehicle load size on each segment of the network k_{12}, k_{23} and k_{31}, are defined by

$$k_{12} = \frac{y_{12} + y_{13} + y_{32}}{f} \qquad k_{23} = \frac{y_{23} + y_{21} + y_{13}}{f} \qquad k_{31} = \frac{y_{31} + y_{32} + y_{21}}{f} \qquad (1.9)$$

Assume arbitrarily that link 1–2 carries the largest load. This can be shown to be equivalent to $y_{12}+y_{13}>y_{21}+y_{31}$ and $y_{12}+y_{32}>y_{21}+y_{23}$. Efficiency implies fully loaded vehicles on that segment, such that $k_{12}=K$. Thus, frequency will be

$$f = \frac{y_{12} + y_{13} + y_{32}}{K} \qquad (1.10)$$

which trivially determines load size on the other two segments according to (1.9). Then, cycle time is given by

$$t_c = \frac{d_{12} + d_{23} + d_{31}}{v} + \frac{2K}{\mu} + \frac{2K}{\mu} \cdot \frac{(y_{21} + y_{23} + y_{31})}{(y_{12} + y_{13} + y_{32})} \qquad (1.11)$$

The production possibility frontier of this route structure is obtained recalling that fleet size B is given by cycle time (equation (1.11)) multiplied by frequency (equation (1.10)), from which

$$BK = (y_{12} + y_{13} + y_{32}) \cdot \left[\frac{d_{12} + d_{23} + d_{31}}{v} + \frac{2K}{\mu} \right] + \frac{2K}{\mu}(y_{21} + y_{23} + y_{31}) \qquad (1.12)$$

with $y_{12} + y_{13} > y_{21} + y_{31}$ and $y_{12} + y_{32} > y_{21} + y_{23}$.

Let us move to a second possible route structure, the one known as *hub-and-spoke*. A hub is a node that collects and distributes all flows, and usually coincides with one that is origin and destination. Let us assume arbitrarily that the hub is in node 2, and that only one fleet (i.e. one frequency) operates. Obviously, other hub-and-spoke structures and more than one fleet could be considered as well, like a two fleet operation, one in 1–2 and the other in 2–3. We have chosen to develop the one fleet structure because the others can be constructed adequately using the two nodes system, as shown below. With our assumption (see Figure 1.5) a vehicle loads flows y_{12} and y_{13} in node 1, unloads y_{12} in 2 and loads y_{23}, then unloads y_{13} and y_{23} in 3, loading y_{32} and y_{31}, goes back to 2 to unload y_{32} and load y_{21} in order to go back to 1 to unload and begin the cycle again.

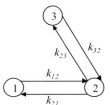

Figure 1.5. *The hub-and-spoke route structure*

In this case, the four load sizes are given by

$$k_{12} = \frac{y_{12} + y_{13}}{f} \qquad k_{32} = \frac{y_{32} + y_{31}}{f}$$

$$k_{23} = \frac{y_{23} + y_{13}}{f} \qquad k_{21} = \frac{y_{31} + y_{21}}{f} \qquad (1.13)$$

Again we will assume total flow in link 1–2 is the largest, which makes k_{12} equal to K and the frequency of the hub-and-spoke system happens to be

$$f = \frac{y_{12} + y_{13}}{K} \qquad (1.14)$$

Replacing (1.14) in (1.13) the other three load sizes are obtained. Cycle time and fleet capacity are calculated as usual, which yields

$$t_c = \frac{d_{12} + d_{23} + d_{32} + d_{21}}{v} + \frac{2K}{\mu} + \frac{2K}{\mu} \cdot \frac{(y_{21} + y_{23} + y_{31} + y_{32})}{(y_{12} + y_{13})} \qquad (1.15)$$

$$BK = (y_{12} + y_{13}) \cdot \left[\frac{d_{12} + d_{23} + d_{32} + d_{21}}{v} + \frac{2K}{\mu} \right] + \frac{2K}{\mu}(y_{21} + y_{23} + y_{31} + y_{32}) \qquad (1.16)$$

For synthesis, the cyclical, backhaul and hub-and-spoke systems are illustrative of the idea of technical feasibility and optimality in transport production. Equations (1.3), (1.8), (1.12) and (1.16) show clearly the relations between inputs and outputs. One of the most important conceptual points is the distinction between inputs, as fleet or loading-unloading capacities, and operating rules, as frequency, speed or vehicle load.

Although roles and relations are clear in the systems examined so far, in more complex systems the technical relations cannot be obtained in such an explicit form. However, they can be envisaged as a sort of 'specialized black box' which includes a number of analytical relations dealing with networks, itineraries, routes, frequencies, and so on, trying to aim at the best possible use of resources. Yet this general idea helps understanding the kernel of transport production; changes in the flow vector *Y* potentially induce changes in input usage as well as in route structures and operating rules in general. It may well be that some of the inputs cannot be adjusted, which means some other inputs will have to be changed in combination with different operating rules. A good example is the restructuring of routes and itineraries for a given fleet of buses facing a change in the passenger volumes in different O - D pairs.

1.2.4. Scale economies

To end this general idea of transport production, let us introduce an important technical concept that can be examined directly from the transformation function: the concept of scale economies, where the relevant question is by how much can output be expanded if all inputs are expanded in the same proportion.

Definition 1.3: Degree of scale economies
The (multioutput) degree of scale economies *S* is defined as the maximum proportional expansion of *Y*, $\lambda^s Y$, after an expansion of the input vector *X* to λX (Panzar and Willig, 1977). Analytically,

$$F\left(\lambda X, \lambda^s Y\right) = 0 \qquad (1.17)$$

A value of *S* greater, equal or smaller than one is called increasing, constant or decreasing returns to scale respectively.

Two and three nodes systems can be viewed from the perspective of scale economies. In the single output case represented by equation (1.3), a local expansion of vehicle capacity (*BK* through *K*) and loading-unloading capacity (μ) would allow *Y* to be increased by the same proportion if speed was unrelated to *K*; note that in this example the right-of-way input is assumed to be exogenous to the firm. In the two-outputs case represented by Figure 1.4 and equation (1.7), a similar expansion of inputs moves the production possibility frontier away from the origin. As the concept of scale economies is forced to deal with proportional expansions of output, it is clear that, again, (y_{12}, y_{21}) can be expanded by the same proportion as inputs (same condition as in the previous case). Note that in the three nodes case, equations (1.12) and (1.16) play a role that is similar to that of (1.7), which shows that the six outputs *can* be expanded by the same proportion So in all these examples *S* takes the value of one; there are constant returns to scale. Note that in all multiple output cases the 'how much can output be expanded' question becomes ambiguous, as nothing has been said about output combinations.

1.3. Transport cost functions: the theory

1.3.1. Basic definitions and properties

Technical analysis is not enough to understand the choice of inputs combination by the firm. The question is which of the combinations in the technical frontier is the most convenient to produce a given output Y. The answer –be it for transport firms or any other– is given by one of the most interesting tools in the microeconomics of production: the cost function, which requires input prices to be introduced in the picture.

Definition 1.4: Cost function
The cost function $C(w,Y)$ gives the minimum expenditure necessary to produce output Y at given factor prices w. It corresponds to the solution of

$$\underset{X}{\text{Min}} \sum_i w_i x_i$$
$$\text{subject to} \qquad F(X,Y) = 0 \tag{1.18}$$

The solution for each input x_i is a conditional demand function $x_i^*(w,Y)$, which represents the optimal amount of input. Then the cost function is

$$C(w,Y) \equiv \sum_i w_i x_i^*(w,Y) \tag{1.19}$$

If some inputs x_j are fixed at a level $\overline{x}_j$, then **the short run cost function is defined as** $C(w_v, \overline{X}, Y)$**, where** $\overline{X}$ **is a vector containing fixed inputs and** w_v **is a vector-containing variable input prices**. The optimization process represented by equations (1.18) and (1.19) is exactly the same.

Following, two well known concepts in microeconomic theory are defined within a multioutput context.

Definition 1.5: Marginal cost
The marginal cost specific to product i, m_i, is defined as

$$m_i = \frac{\partial C(w,Y)}{\partial y_i} \tag{1.20}$$

Definition 1.6: Cost elasticity
The cost elasticity with respect to output i, η_i, is

$$\eta_i = \frac{y_i}{C(w,Y)} \frac{\partial C(w,Y)}{\partial y_i} \tag{1.21}$$

Out of the many properties of the cost function two are particularly relevant for a basic analysis and discussion of production in general and of transport in particular:

Property 1.1: Shephard's lemma
The derivative property or Shephard's lemma states that the derivative of the cost function $C(w,Y)$ with respect to each factor input price w_i equals the cost minimizing amount of x_i, that is $x_i^*(w, Y)$. Analytically,

$$\frac{\partial C(w,Y)}{\partial w_i} \equiv x_i^*(w,Y) \tag{1.22}$$

This is very helpful in estimating and interpreting a cost function, because the huge number of parameters to be estimated associated to the usage of flexible forms of the cost function, requires a very large number of observations for statistical confidence. The application of (1.22) generates additional equations involving subsets of the original parameters, which improves the efficiency of the estimates.

Property 1.2: Scale Economies
If S is defined as in (1.17) it can be calculated as (Panzar and Willig, 1977)

$$S = \frac{C(Y)}{\sum_i y_i \frac{\partial C}{\partial y_i}} = \frac{1}{\sum_i \eta_i} \tag{1.23}$$

where η_i is the cost elasticity with respect to output i (see appendix for a proof). In other words, the multioutput degree of scale economies S defined in (1.17) can be calculated from the cost function. Note that S is given by the ratio between average and marginal cost in the single output case.

In the case of multiple outputs, the analysis of industry structure requires something more than the study of production *scale*. Additional information is required in terms of the convenience of producing two or more outputs together; scope economies:

Definition 1.7: Degree of economies of scope
The degree of economies of scope relative to a subset R, SC_R, is defined as (Baumol et al., 1982)

$$SC_R = \frac{1}{C(Y)} [C(Y_R) + C(Y_{M-R}) - C(Y)] \tag{1.24}$$

where Y_R represents vector Y with $y_i = 0, \forall i \notin R \subset M$, with M being the set of all products (we have suppressed w for simplicity). Thus, a positive SC_R -the existence of economies of scope- means that it is cheaper to produce Y with a single firm than having two firms, one producing the subset R and the other the subset $M\text{-}R$. Note that SC_R lies, theoretically, in the interval $[-1,1]$, as it represents the proportion of cost savings due to joint production.

If we want to know the cost of adding a subset R to its complement $M\text{-}R$ of the total product Y, we have to calculate the incremental cost:

Definition 1.8: Incremental cost
The incremental cost relative to a subset R, IC_R, is calculated as

$$IC_R = C(Y) - C(Y_{M\text{-}R}) \tag{1.25}$$

The concept of a natural monopoly within a multioutput framework is equivalent to the presence of *subadditivity* in the cost function

Definition 1.9: Subadditive cost function
A cost function is said to be subadditive for a particular output vector Y when Y can be produced at a lower cost by a single firm than by any combination of smaller firms (Baumol *et. al.*, 1982, p. 170). Therefore, a cost function is subadditive if

$$\sum_i C(Y^i) \geq C(Y) \qquad \forall \{Y^i\} \text{ such that } \sum_i Y^i = Y \tag{1.26}$$

Under this set of definitions and properties, it is very clear that both $S>1$ and $SC_R>0$ favor subadditivity, but neither guarantees its presence by itself.

Definition 1.10: Degree of scale economies for a subset R
The degree of scale economies for a subset R is

$$S_R = \frac{IC_R}{\sum_{i \in R} y_i \dfrac{\partial C}{\partial y_i}} \tag{1.27}$$

Property 1.3: Relation between Scale Economies and Scope
Overall scale economies, scope and scale economies for a subset $R \subset M$ are related, since

$$S = \frac{S_R \alpha_R + S_{M-R}(1-\alpha_R)}{1 - SC_R(Y)} \tag{1.28}$$

$$\text{with} \quad \alpha_R = \frac{\sum_{i \in R} y_i \frac{\partial C}{\partial y_i}}{\sum_{i \in M} y_i \frac{\partial C}{\partial y_i}}$$

Proof.
Replacing (1.25) in (1.24) we get

$$SC_R = \frac{1}{C(Y)} \left[C(Y) - IC_R - IC_{M-R} \right] \tag{1.29}$$

From (1.23)

$$C(Y) = S \sum_i y_i \frac{\partial C}{\partial y_i} \tag{1.30}$$

Replacing this in (1.29) and using (1.27) and the definition of α_R we get

$$SC_R = \frac{1}{S} \left[S - \alpha_R S_R - \alpha_{M-R} S_{M-R} \right] \tag{1.31}$$

Finally, noting that $\alpha_{M-R} = 1 - \alpha_R$ we get (1.28).

Property 1.3 means S would be a weighted average of S_R and S_{M-R} in the absence of economies of scope. If these exist, S is magnified.

1.3.2. Scale and scope in transport production

The preceding section, valid for all types of firms, is of course applicable to a transport one. With product defined as in equation (1.1) and the notion of scale synthesized in equation (1.17), scale analysis in transport should be conceptually clear: **scale in transport refers to the behavior of costs as flows in *all markets* served by a firm expand proportionally.** On the other hand, following the notion of scope introduced in equation (1.24), **scope analysis in transport refers to the behavior of costs when flows are separated into two mutually exclusive subsets.** In order to emphasize space, let us create an example using the O-D structure depicted in Figure 1.1 for one type of cargo.

Example 1.2
In Figure 1.1 and Figure 1.2 imagine that flows y_{ij} and y_{ji} are unbalanced, and that the sum of flows clockwise is approximately equal to the sum of flows counter-clockwise. It may well be that for relatively low volumes, a service structure like a), with complete vehicle cycles involving a homogeneous fleet, is the minimum cost answer. Imagine output expands proportionally as required by scale analysis; the firm could accommodate that expansion by increasing frequency (expanding fleet) and/or using larger vehicles. For

further expansions, the hub-and-spoke structure like b) could well become the best answer, making the hub a transfer point and including vehicles of different sizes. It might be the case that direct services like in c) happen to be the minimum cost structure for individually large enough flows. If there are scale advantages in loading-unloading activities and in vehicle size, it is very likely that through appropriate scheduling and rerouting, total cost will increase less than proportionally with increases in the flow vector, at least up to a certain scale.

Regarding scope, Figure 1.1 again will prove very helpful. If the six flows are divided into subsets $\{y_{12}, y_{23}, y_{31}\}$ and $\{y_{21}, y_{13}, y_{32}\}$, very possibly the sum of the costs of assigning each subset to a different firm will be greater than that cost of moving all six flows with one firm. The case is not that clear when the partition is $\{y_{12}, y_{21}\},\{y_{13}, y_{31}, y_{23}, y_{32}\}$. In general, the partition of the flow vector could be made in terms of flow type (for example passengers and freight), periods (for example weekends and weekdays) or O-D pairs, as we have done in the example. In this latter case we would talk about economies of spatial scope, when they exist.

In order to provide a specific analytical case, let us use the simple backhaul system to obtain and analyze the corresponding cost function. To get total expenses in the production of a given vector Y, input prices have to be considered. Let g be vehicle fuel consumption per kilometer, ε and θ the number of men required to operate a vehicle and a loading/unloading site respectively, w the wage rate, P_g the fuel price, P_K and P_μ the price per hour of a vehicle of capacity K and the price per hour of a loading/unloading site of capacity μ respectively (consider these either as rental prices or depreciation). To simplify matters, let g be independent of load size and speed, let ε and θ be independent of K and μ respectively, and consider the case of $y_{12} > y_{21}$. With these assumptions and variable definitions, vehicle expenses per hour including rent and operation (labor and fuel) are given by

$$P_{veh} = P_K + w \cdot \varepsilon + P_g \cdot g \cdot \frac{d_{12} + d_{21}}{B \cdot K} y_{12} \tag{1.32}$$

Regarding loading/unloading sites, the expense per hour P_S and the number of sites needed NS are given respectively by

$$P_S = P_\mu + w\theta \tag{1.33}$$

$$NS = \frac{2(y_{12} + y_{21})}{\mu} \tag{1.34}$$

Next, total expenses G can be calculated as the sum of the payments for the right-of-way C_0, for the vehicles (B times P_{veh}), and for the loading/unloading sites (NS times P_S). Thus, from equations (1.32), (1.33) and (1.34) we get

$$G_{K,\mu,\nu}(y_{12},y_{21})=C_0+\left[P_K+w\varepsilon\right]\cdot B(K,\mu,\nu,Y)+\frac{P_g\cdot g\cdot(d_{12}+d_{21})}{K}y_{12}+\frac{2\cdot P_S\cdot(y_{12}+y_{21})}{\mu} \quad (1.35)$$

Assuming vehicles and sites are available in a given size only, and that speed is exogenously determined by technical or legal facts, K, μ and ν are fixed and the optimal fleet size B^* for a given product Y is directly given by equation (1.7), which replaced in equation (1.35) yields the cost function

$$C(y_{12},y_{21})=C_0+y_{12}(d_{12}+d_{21})\cdot\Lambda+(y_{12}+y_{21})\cdot\Omega \quad (1.36)$$

with $\qquad \Lambda=\left[\dfrac{P_K+w\varepsilon}{\nu K}+\dfrac{P_g g}{K}\right] \qquad$ and $\qquad \Omega=\left[\dfrac{2}{\mu}(P_K+w\varepsilon)+\dfrac{2P_S}{\mu}\right]$

with a symmetric expression for $y_{21}>y_{12}$.[1] This cost function is represented in Figure 1.6.

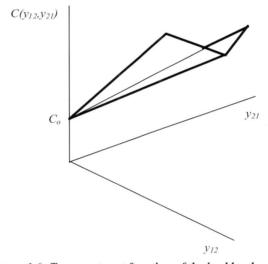

Figure 1.6. *Transport cost function of the backhaul system*

It is interesting to note that equation (1.36) includes a flow-distance term and a pure flow term. Following Jara-Díaz (1982b), the latter captures those expenses that occur while product is not in motion, i.e. those due to terminal operations (as is evident through Ω), while the flow-distance term captures en-route expenses (evidently reflected by Λ). This is graphically represented in Figure 1.6. Note that the flow-distance term is, in fact, the capacity of the transport system, as only the largest flow appears –i.e. the one that equals

---

[1] A complete analytical derivation of cost functions for both the simple cyclical system and the backhaul system can be found in Jara-Díaz (1982b).

frequency multiplied by vehicle capacity– and is multiplied by the total distance traveled by each vehicle.

Although equation (1.36) has been obtained using highly simplifying assumptio ns, it represents a fairly transparent cost function for the simplest possible multioutput trans port system. Its importance becomes apparent when it is used to analyze scale, scope and aggregate output. If the degree of economies of scale is calculated using (1.23), it is quite easy to show that

$$S = \frac{C(y_{12}, y_{21})}{|C(y_{12}, y_{21}) - C_0|} \qquad \forall (y_{12}, y_{21}) \tag{1.37}$$

In particular, $S=1$ for $C_0 = 0$, which we can name the 'truck' case, as trucks (or buses) do not pay a fixed cost for road infrastructure. On the other hand, scope analysis can be done for the only partition possible in this case (i.e. assigning each of the flows in the backhaul system to differ ent firms). After elementary calculations we get

$$C(y_{12}, 0) + C(0, y_{21}) - C(y_{12}, y_{21}) = C_o + y_{ji}(d_{12} + d_{21}) \cdot \Lambda \qquad \forall y_{ij} \geq y_{ji} \tag{1.38}$$

which is positive even if C_o is nil. This shows that, under the assumptions made, it is fleet utilization what causes the existence of economies of scope, that is, production of (y_{12}, y_{21}) is cheaper with one firm than with two or more firms producing orthogonal partitions of that output bundle. Thus, if $C_o=0$, we have constant returns (a case for competition or deregulation) and economies of scope. The latter would cause incentives for merging if two firms are operating, each in one direction. The conclusion is that, as far as costs of production are concerned, competition would be desirable but each firm should operate serving both markets.

1.3.3. The conditional and global cost functions: the role of flows and network

As stated earlier, the decisions of a transport firm are three: quantity and characteristics of inputs, operating rules and route structure. Given the discrete nature of the latter decision, the underlying cost minimizing process can be seen as a sequence with two stages. First, **for a given route structure** the firm optimizes inputs and operating rules. After establishing the production possibility frontier (technical optimality) input prices are considered and expenses are minimized. A **conditional cost function**, that gives the minimum cost necessary to produce a given output Y for given output prices and a known route structure, is obtained. In the second stage these conditional cost functions (corresponding to alternative route structures) are compared and the global cost function can be obtained by choosing the cost minimizing route structure. Note the two nodes system is insufficient to show the two stages optimization process completely, as the second stage is not applicable to this single route structure case. However, this case will prove very useful for the explanation of the three nodes system -where a choice on route structure indeed exists- and for the comparison of costs after a network expansion, as developed by Jara-Díaz and Basso (2003).

Let us derive the conditional cost function for the three nodes system, for two different service structures. In the case of a general cyclical counter-clockwise structure (Figure 1.2.a), given K, μ and v, equation (1.12) is directly $B^*(Y)$. Just as we did with the two nodes system, the (conditional) cost function is obtained calculating expenses per vehicle-hour times B^*, and adding loading-unloading sites expenses plus the right-of-way cost. Doing this and after some manipulation, we get

$$C_{CG}(Y) = C_0 + (y_{12} + y_{13} + y_{32}) \cdot (d_{12} + d_{23} + d_{31}) \cdot \Lambda + (y_{12} + y_{13} + y_{32} + y_{21} + y_{31} + y_{23}) \cdot \Omega$$
(1.39)

$$\text{with} \quad y_{12} + y_{13} > y_{21} + y_{31} \quad \text{and} \quad y_{12} + y_{32} > y_{21} + y_{23} \,.$$

This is the cost function conditional on a cyclical route structure, with Λ and Ω defined as in equation (1.36). The similarity between this conditional cost function and the one obtained for the two nodes system equation (1.36) is evident. Note the obtained function reduces to that of the two nodes system if the four new flows are set to zero and $d_{23} + d_{31}$ was defined as d_{21}.

Following the same procedure as in the previous case, we obtain the conditional cost function in the hub-and-spoke route structure, i.e.

$$C_{HS}(Y) = C_0 + (y_{12} + y_{13}) \cdot (d_{12} + d_{23} + d_{32} + d_{21}) \cdot \Lambda + (y_{12} + y_{13} + y_{32} + y_{21} + y_{31} + y_{23}) \cdot \Omega$$
(1.40)

whose terms have the same interpretation as the ones in equation (1.39).

So far, we have obtained two conditional cost functions for the three nodes system. By simple analogy, the conditional functions for other three route structures can be obtained as well: the clockwise cyclical system and the hub-and-spoke systems with the hub in nodes 1 or 3. Additionally, by adequately using the cost function for the two nodes system, we can derive conditional cost functions for other cases: the direct service with three fleets, each one serving a pair of nodes cyclically (1-2, 2-3 and 1-3), and the hub-and-spoke with two fleets, each one connecting a pair of nodes (with the hub at any of the three nodes). Note that in this latter case some flows will have to be loaded and unloaded twice (origin, destination and hub), which increases expenses compared with the other cases, but cycle times will be shorter. The examples developed and explained here are enough to illustrate that choosing a route structure is a key endogenous element, and to show that the minimum cost is associated with such choice.

The second stage of the sequential optimization process is the search for the optimal route structure, i.e. the one that minimizes cost in the production of Y and defines the global cost function. This second stage requires the comparison of the conditional cost functions obtained in the first stage. Let us illustrate this process in the three nodes system considering $y_{ij} = y$ (equal flows) and the network shown in Figure 1.7.

Transport Economic Theory

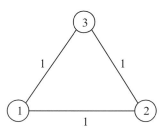

Figure 1.7. *Physical network*

Let us define the following notation for the alternative route structures:

CG-123 : Cyclic counter-clockwise.
CG-132 : Cyclic clockwise.
3F   : Direct Service; three fleets.
HS-i   : Hub-and-spoke with the hub in node *i*; one fleet.
2F-i   : Hub-and-spoke with the hub in node *i*; two fleets.

Using the conditional cost functions explicitly derived earlier and the definitions of the systems, the conditional cost function for each of nine route structures can be constructed and evaluated for the equilateral triangular network in Figure 1.7 and equal flows on each O-D pair. Omitting C_0 for simplicity the results are

$$
\begin{aligned}
C_{CG\text{-}123} = C_{CG\text{-}132} &= 9 \cdot y \cdot \Lambda + 6 \cdot y \cdot \Omega \\
C_{HS\text{-}1} = C_{HS\text{-}2} = C_{HS\text{-}3} &= 8 \cdot y \cdot \Lambda + 6 \cdot y \cdot \Omega \\
C_{3F} &= 6 \cdot y \cdot \Lambda + 6 \cdot y \cdot \Omega \\
C_{2F\text{-}1} = C_{2F\text{-}2} = C_{2F\text{-}3} &= 8 \cdot y \cdot \Lambda + 8 \cdot y \cdot \Omega
\end{aligned}
\tag{1.41}
$$

Thus, it is optimum to serve the flows directly with three fleets, each one connecting a pair of nodes. Therefore, this is the global cost function for this particular network with equal distances and equal flows. It is worth noting that the hub-and-spoke structures with two fleets have larger costs than the ones with one fleet because of terminal operations, and that the cyclic systems have the largest en-route costs.

The choice of a route structure is dependant on exogenous information, namely the O-D structure of demand (vector *Y*) and the network topology. Let us examine the effect of a variation of this exogenous information on the choice of an optimal route structure. First, let us see the effect of changes in O-D structure of demand, keeping the same physical network (**flow effect**). Consider the O-D structure represented in Figure 1.8.

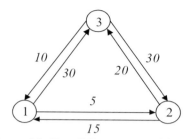

Figure 1.8. *New O-D structure of demand*

Now flows are asymmetric, which forces to identify the flows that generate the largest load size, as these are the ones multiplying Λ. With these new values for the components of Y, the (conditional) cost for each of the nine proposed route structures are:

$$
\begin{aligned}
C_{CG\text{-}123} &= 195{\cdot}\Lambda + 110{\cdot}\Omega & C_{HS\text{-}1} &= 200{\cdot}\Lambda + 110{\cdot}\Omega & C_{2F\text{-}1} &= 170{\cdot}\Lambda + 160{\cdot}\Omega \\
C_{CG\text{-}132} &= 165{\cdot}\Lambda + 110{\cdot}\Omega & C_{HS\text{-}2} &= 200{\cdot}\Lambda + 110{\cdot}\Omega & C_{2F\text{-}2} &= 170{\cdot}\Lambda + 150{\cdot}\Omega \\
C_{3F} &= 150{\cdot}\Lambda + 110{\cdot}\Omega & C_{HS\text{-}3} &= 140{\cdot}\Lambda + 110{\cdot}\Omega & C_{2F\text{-}3} &= 140{\cdot}\Lambda + 130{\cdot}\Omega
\end{aligned}
\tag{1.42}
$$

The new optimal route structure is the hub-and-spoke with one fleet and the hub located in node 3, $C_{HS\text{-}3}$. This shows that a different O-D structure can generate a new optimal route structure on the same physical network (spatial distribution of nodes and link lengths).

Let us change the network as shown in Figure 1.9, but keeping the O-D structure of Figure 1.8 in order to examine the **network effect**.

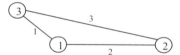

Figure 1.9. *New network: spatial distribution of nodes and link lengths*

The new conditional costs functions are:

$$
\begin{aligned}
C_{CG\text{-}123} &= 390{\cdot}\Lambda + 110{\cdot}\Omega & C_{HS\text{-}1} &= 300{\cdot}\Lambda + 110{\cdot}\Omega & C_{2F\text{-}1} &= 240{\cdot}\Lambda + 160{\cdot}\Omega \\
C_{CG\text{-}132} &= 330{\cdot}\Lambda + 110{\cdot}\Omega & C_{HS\text{-}2} &= 500{\cdot}\Lambda + 110{\cdot}\Omega & C_{2F\text{-}2} &= 440{\cdot}\Lambda + 150{\cdot}\Omega \\
C_{3F} &= 300{\cdot}\Lambda + 110{\cdot}\Omega & C_{HS\text{-}3} &= 280{\cdot}\Lambda + 110{\cdot}\Omega & C_{2F\text{-}3} &= 280{\cdot}\Lambda + 130{\cdot}\Omega
\end{aligned}
\tag{1.43}
$$

Unlike the previous cases, now the optimal route structure depends on the values of Λ and Ω. The *HS-3* system (which was the best with the previous network) is still superior to both cyclic systems, to *3F*, to the other hub-and-spoke systems and to the two fleet systems but *2F-1*. However, the hub-and-spoke system with two fleets and the hub in node 1 could be superior to *HS-3* depending on the relative values of Λ and Ω, which are constants defined mostly by prices. Thus, the decision on the optimal route structure will depend, in this case, on how expensive are the loading/unloading activities relative to activities en-route, which is very reasonable. Note that a proportional growth of distances (links) would increase the difference between expenses en-route of the two structures, keeping the difference between terminal expenses constant, which would increase the attractiveness of route structure *2F-1*. This illustrates the network effect on the optimal route structure.

Regarding scale analysis in the three nodes system, it is quite simple to show that for all the conditional cost functions the degree of economies of scale S is given by equation (1.37) due to linearity in flows. Then $C_0 = 0$ implies constant returns and $C_0 > 0$ generates increasing returns.

The analysis of scope allows various possible orthogonal partitions of the six flows product vector (Figure 1.1.a). It is particularly interesting to analyze the case in which one node is added or subtracted from a firm service (network expansion or reduction). Let us consider the orthogonal partition $Y_R = \{y_{12}, y_{21}, 0, 0, 0, 0\}$, $Y_{M-R} = \{0, 0, y_{13}, y_{31}, y_{23}, y_{32}\}$, which allows the comparison between one firm serving all six flows against two firms, one serving the two flows between nodes 1 and 2 and the other serving the rest. Note $C(Y)$-$C(Y_R)$ is precisely the cost caused by the addition of node 3 to the network $\{1,2\}$, not necessarily equal to $C(Y_{M-R})$ unless SC_R was nil. As seen, the value of the degree of economies of scope depends on the exogenous information (flows and network) because the global cost function does. We will analyze the case depicted in Figure 1.8 with link lengths equal to one, with $C_0 = 0$ in order to get rid of the fixed cost effect that influences (increases) both scale and scope. In this case, the global cost function for the firm serving all flows corresponds to that of the *HS-3* structure, which yields $C(Y)=140 \cdot \Lambda + 110 \cdot \Omega$. On the other hand, the global cost function for the two flows system is given by equation (1.36), which yields $C(Y_R) = 30 \cdot \Lambda + 20 \cdot \Omega$. For Y_{M-R}, the three nodes system analysis applies, with two flows set to zero. It can be shown that the optimal route structure could be either *2F-3* or *HS-3*, both with a cost $C(Y_{M-R})$ given by $120 \cdot \Lambda + 90 \cdot \Omega$. Now we can calculate SC_R from equation (1.24), which yields

$$SC_R = \frac{(30\,\Lambda + 20\,\Omega) + (120\,\Lambda + 90\,\Omega) - (140\,\Lambda + 110\,\Omega)}{C(Y)} = \frac{10 \cdot \Lambda}{C(Y)} > 0 \qquad (1.44)$$

This means that, even if $C_0=0$, the six flows will be better served with one firm. Note that in this case savings occur due to expenses en-route, i.e. a single firm allows a better use of the fleet capacity than two firms (vehicle load is larger in average) by means of adjustments in the route structure. Note also this might not happen for other values of Y or for another physical network. The same applies to loading/unloading activities; in this particular case they are neither a source of economies nor diseconomies of scope because in the three optimal route structures every unit is loaded and unloaded once. Under other circumstances, a hub-and-spoke structure with two fleets might be optimal in producing Y, with loading and unloading activities being a source of diseconomies of spatial scope.

1.4. Transport cost functions: the empirical work

1.4.1. Transport output and the estimation of cost functions

The estimation of cost functions for different transport industries has been the preferred tool to analyze the role of the cost structure in the organization of the industry, as well as regulation, technical change, productivity, and so on. But obtaining an adequate representation of either $C(w,Y)$ or $C(w,\overline{X},Y)$ -the long run and the short run cost functions respectively- is not a simple task. Evidently, the general idea is to construct a reliable statistical relation between expenses as the dependent variable, and output, input prices and fixed factors as explanatory variables. The statistical data is composed by a series of observations, each one relating production to cost. This series can be fed by:

- the evolution of a single transport firm in time (time series);

- the activity of many firms within a period (cross section);

- observations of many firms during many periods (pool).

The case of a time series is, conceptually speaking, the most transparent one because it refers to one firm, one O-D structure and one network; product (as defined in equation (1.1) is quite precise, as well as factors of production.

Example 1.3
Let us consider the case of a firm moving a single type of commodity (or passengers) among many points in space during homogeneous periods, and imagine potential observations that include services from two to six O-D pairs as depicted in Figure 1.10. If all observations were associated with an O-D system like (a), output would be a two-dimensional vector. Output would be a six-dimensional vector if *all* observations were related with movements like those represented in (c).

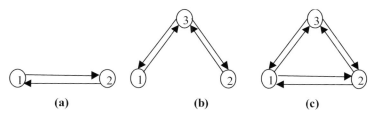

(a)   (b)   (c)

Figure 1.10. *Transport output in a three nodes system*

How to represent output if observations included all three cases? The answer is straightforward: the output vector should have six components and some of them will be nil for observations including flows like in (a) or (b). Formally, denoting y_{ij}^n the actual flow in O-D pair ij for observation (period) n,

$$y = \{y_{12}, y_{21}, y_{13}, y_{31}, y_{23}, y_{32}\}$$

$$Y^A = \left\{ y^a_{12}, y^a_{21}, 0, 0, 0, 0 \right\}$$

$$Y^B = \left\{ 0, 0, y^b_{13}, y^b_{31}, y^b_{23}, y^b_{32} \right\}$$

$$Y^C = \left\{ y^c_{12}, y^f_{21}, y^c_{13}, y^c_{31}, y^f_{23}, y^f_{32} \right\}$$

The case is very similar if observations correspond to transport firms operating on the same spatial setting.

Observations of firms serving different O-D pairs correspond, in fact, to different products. This does make a difference regarding other production processes observed through a cross-section, as the optimal combination of resources to produce a given amount of an output bundle (say shoes, bags and belts) at given input prices, is likely to be equal across firms if all of them have access to the same technology. But the optimal combination of vehicles, terminals and rights-of-way (by means of routes, frequencies and load sizes) will depend upon the characteristics of the underlying physical network and the actual configuration of each O-D system. Nevertheless, it is true that an external observer (transport analyst) should be able to obtain some information regarding cost structure from observations of different transport firms performing similar services on different spatial settings (for example interurban rail, urban transit, international flights, and so on). But this requires a careful analysis in order to make the correct inferences on policy and industry structure.

Thus, transport output description within the context of the estimation of cost functions, implies a challenge at least in two dimensions. First, when output is well defined as a vector of O-D flows, the number of components is usually huge and certainly unmanageable in detail for statistical purposes. Second, cross-sectional observations usually involve different products in a spatial sense. How to aggregate flow components and how to introduce product equivalency or homogeneity across different systems, are indeed problems to solve (Jara-Díaz *et al.*, 1991, 1992); neither, however, changes the strict definitions of scale and scope which are unambiguous with a well defined transport output.

1.4.2. Functional form

From 1970 to 2000, the empirical work on transport cost functions has experienced a series of improvements. Perhaps the most evident is the use of flexible forms for the functional specification of the function, with the translog form being the most popular (see Christensen *et al.*, 1973). In order to understand analytically this form, it is useful to view first another flexible specification called the quadratic. Conceptually, the quadratic corresponds to a second order Taylor expansion of $C(w, Y)$ around a point (w^0, Y^0), which is usually the mean of input prices $(\overline{w}_i)$ and flows $(\overline{y}_i)$ in the data set. Analytically, the stochastic expression for the quadratic-around-the-mean cost function is

$$C(w,Y) = A_0 + \sum_{i=1}^{n} A_i(w_i - \overline{w}_i) + \sum_{i=1}^{m} C_i(y_i - \overline{y}_i)$$

$$+\frac{1}{2}\sum_{i=1}^{n}\sum_{j=1}^{n} A_{ij}(w_i - \overline{w}_i)(w_j - \overline{w}_j)$$

$$+\frac{1}{2}\sum_{i=1}^{n}\sum_{j=1}^{m} B_{ij}(w_i - w_j)(y_j - \overline{y}_j) \tag{1.45}$$

$$+\frac{1}{2}\sum_{i=1}^{m}\sum_{j=1}^{n} C_{ij}(y_i - \overline{y}_i)(y_j - \overline{y}_j) + \varepsilon,$$

where the system considers n inputs and m outputs; ε is an error tem. The translog form is analogous to equation (1.45) with $C(w, Y)$, w_i and y_i (including deviation points) in logs. Both forms are flexible in the sense that no a priori functions are postulated either for technology or costs.

Each of these flexible forms has its own advantages. The translog facilitates the analysis of the properties corresponding to the underlying technology, i.e. homogeneity, separability, scale economies and non-joint production, by means of relatively simple tests on the adequate set of parameter estimates.[2] Its first order coefficients are the cost elasticities of output calculated at the mean, and their summation yields an estimate of the inverse of S as shown in equation (1.23).

On the other hand, the plain quadratic form is extremely adequate to directly obtain marginal costs evaluated at the mean of observations, C_i and the elements of the Hessian C_{ij}, which are essential for analyzing subadditivity. In addition, equation (1.45) is well defined for zero output levels (while the translog is not); this not only represents an advantage for the estimation process, but also allows for the calculation of economies of scope, which involve output vectors with some zero components. Nevertheless, adequate transformations of output (for example Box-Cox) allow for nil values of output using the translog form as well.

One of the shortcomings of flexible forms is the fairly high number of coefficients to be estimated, which requires a substantially larger number of observations for statistical relevance. However, the application of Sheppard's Lemma to equation (1.45) generates as many additional equations as factor prices included, involving part of the coefficients from the original equation. Inputting some usually available information (factor usage, factor expenditure or factor cost share)[3] the number of 'observations' can be multiplied,

---

[2] For a condensed overview of the technical analysis based upon the coefficients obtained from the translog specification of $C(w, Y)$, see Spady and Friedlaender (1978).

[3] As Shephard's Lemma states that $\dfrac{\partial C(w,Y)}{\partial w_i} = X_i$, this can be manipulated to obtain either $w_i\dfrac{\partial C}{\partial w_i}$ (factor expenditure) or $\dfrac{w_i}{C}\dfrac{\partial C}{\partial w_i}$ (factor share). This last form is particularly appropriate when using the translog form.

generating a system of equations which increases the parameter estimation efficiency. This problem is particularly relevant in transport analysis because the usually high dimension of Y is further magnified by squared and interaction terms.

A widely used way to deal with the large number of variables when estimating cost functions is representing output by means of aggregates, a procedure that has its own problems, as we will see next.

1.4.3. Output aggregates

Since output is usually a vector of huge dimensions, the empirical literature shows a variety of aggregate output indices that, placed in groups of three or four, are used for the estimation of cost functions in an effort to capture the complexity of transport services.

But aggregation over any dimension (commodity, time or space) involves loosing information associated with the transport processes generated by the system in reference. Clearly, spatial aggregation destroys information on the geographical context of the origin-destination system in which a transport system operates. Aggregation of output over time may cause distortions when estimating cost functions if periods of distinctive mean flows are being averaged. Finally, commodity aggregation may affect cost estimation since the (minimum) cost of moving the same aggregate weight or volume will generally depend on the composition of that output.

Despite these problems, even to date aggregates like passenger- (or ton-) kilometers *(TK)* are used as a basic or synthetic unit to describe transport output both in general and within the context of empirically estimated cost functions. Since the late seventies, its ambiguity began to be addressed, raising issues like network shape and fleet utilization. The usual critique to the *TK* aggregate is that it is different, both in terms of inputs and cost, to move n tons across m kilometers from moving m tons across n kilometers. But this is far from being the only problem.

Example 1.4
The simplified cost function of the backhaul system can be used to illustrate the limitations of the *TK* index as a representation of transport output. First we have to recognize that *TK* is indeed a function of the true output as defined in (1.1). In the backhaul system,

$$TK = y_{12}d_{12} + y_{21}d_{21} \tag{1.46}$$

On the other hand, equation (1.36) can be used to represent the combinations of y_{12} and y_{21} that yield the same expenditure C_i. The resulting iso-cost locus can be shown in the output space as we have done in Figure 1.11, where cost increases with the distance from the origin. The popular 'output' *TK* can be shown in the same space using equation (1.46) as a straight line with a negative slope that depends on the relative value of d_{12} and d_{21}. Evidently, all flow combinations within the straight line yield the same value for *TK*. We have represented as TK_o the case of $d_{12} > d_{21}$; as the corresponding line intersects many iso-cost curves, TK_o cannot be associated with a single minimum cost figure. If should be noted that this ambiguity remains even if both distances were equal (as represented by TK_1). On the other hand, every pair (y_{12}, y_{21}) corresponds to a single cost value, unambiguously.

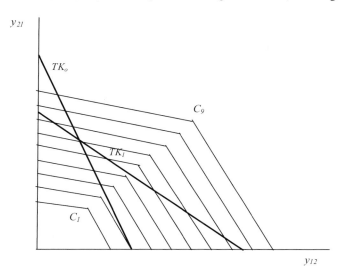

Figure 1.11. *Cost ambiguity of aggregate output*

In terms of scale analysis, an expansion of TK by λ corresponds to several possible flow combinations, as shown by equation (1.46). In terms of scope, the pairs $(0, y_{21})$ and $(y_{12}, 0)$ get reflected as $y_{21} d_{21}$ and $y_{12} d_{12}$ respectively when converted into TK units. Thus, scope 'turns' into scale, provoking an extremely confusing panorama when trying to obtain conclusions on industry structure.

The ambiguity of aggregate output is a key aspect in the analysis of industry structure in transport activities by means of a cost function. With an example we have shown that, even in a simple system like the backhaul service, an association between expenses C and output TK might yield completely erroneous conclusions. Even so, reported transport cost functions use a basic output aggregate (such as ton-kilometers or total passenger trips) together with other 'output' variables or, as called in the literature, 'output characteristics'. These other aggregates aim at somehow control for the ambiguity of the single output index. Thus, seasonal and 'traffic condition' dummies are in fact trying to capture the effect of the implicit time aggregation on costs. Similarly, variables like traffic mix or insurance value try to grasp commodity aggregation. The first effort to somehow counterbalance spatial aggregation was the use of mean haul length as part of output description within a 'hedonic' treatment (Spady and Friedlaender, 1978). Up to date, the literature on transport cost functions includes an enormous variety of output descriptions. Unfortunately, this has not led yet to a universally accepted form of output treatment, mainly due to an implicit reluctance to try to understand transport technology, which is a fairly complex construct as suggested at the beginning of the chapter. In order to clarify this, let us use the synthesis presented in Table 1.1, where we have included studies covering more than twenty years of evaluation. [4]

Table 1.1. Output description in transport cost functions

	MODE	OUTPUT	ATTRIBUTE
Berechman (1983)	bus	REV	
Berechman (1987) Berechman and Giuliano (1984)	bus	VK, PAS	
Ying (1990) Ying *et al.* (1991)	trucks	RTK	ALH, %LTL, AL, AS, IN
Caves *et al.* (1984) Gillen *et al.* (1990) Windle (1991) Liu and Lynk (1999) Creel and Farell (2001)	air	RPK Scheduled services RTK Charter services	ALH or ASL, LF, NC
Daughety *et al.* (1985) Friedlaender and Bruce (1985) Kim (1987) (*) Spady and Friedlaender (1978) Wang and Friedlaender (1984)	trucks	TK	ALH, AS, AL, %LTL, IN, CU
Gagné (1990)	trucks	TK, N	ALH, AS, CU, IN
Caves *et al.* (1980, 1981, 1985)	rail	TK, PK	ALH, ATL
Filippini and Maggi (1992) Formby et. al. (1990) Keeler and Formby (1994) Tauchen *et al.* (1983) Koshal and Koshal (1989) Braeutigam *et al.* (1980) Keaton (1990)	air bus trucks railways	SK, VK, LCK	LF, ALH, TD, NC
Harmatuck (1981, 1985, 1991)	trucks	NTL, NLTL	ALH, ASTL, ASLTL

TK:	ton-kilometers	%LTL:	percentage of less-than-truckload services
PK:	passenger-kilometers	AL:	average load
PAS:	passengers-trips	AS:	average shipment size
RTK:	revenue ton-kilometers	IN:	average cargo loss-and-damage insurance per dollar of cost
RPK:	revenue pax-kilometers	LF:	load factor
REV:	revenue per pax-kilometer	CU:	capacity utilization
VK:	vehicle-kilometers	TD:	traffic density
SK:	seat-kilometers	NC:	network characteristics (for example points served, hub, etc.)
LCK:	loaded car-kilometers	ALH:	average length of haul (freight)
NTL:	number of truckload shipments	ATL:	average trip length (passengers)
NLTL:	number of less-than-truckload shipments	ASL:	average stage length
N:	number of shipments	ASTL:	average shipment size (truckload)
		ASLTL:	average shipment size (less-than-truckload)

---

[4] Note this is not intended as a review of techniques and results. The reader might want to look at two fairly complete studies: the period 1970-1980 is reviewed in detail in Jara-Díaz, 1982a; the period 1980-1996 is analyzed by Oumand Waters (1996).

From Table 1.1 we can verify that in addition to full aggregation of flows (for example passengers) or distance-weighted flows (for example ton-kilometers), the list of accompanying variables is varied: average load, average trip length, percentage of less-than-truckload services, number of shipments, average shipment size, etcetera. It is important to note that these variables are sometimes called outputs, sometimes output characteristics, and sometimes quality dimensions. The most sophisticated variables appeared during the eighties, and they are related with network shape and size. And here we have a new source of confusion: network as infrastructure, (i.e. a fixed factor associated with the rights-of-way) and network as route structure, which is an endogenous, operating decision for many modes or transport systems (for example the cyclical system or the hub-and-spoke in Figure 1.2; see Jara-Díaz and Basso, 2003).

The use of aggregates poses a relevant problem. Transport production is a multioutput process where the concepts of scale and scope are very useful for the analysis of industry structure, provided they are properly applied. As seen, the degree of economies of scale reflects the behavior of cost as all flows (e.g. in every O-D pair) expand proportionally. The degree of economies of scope examines the convenience of partitioning transport services into two mutually exclusive subsets; depending on the type of partition, we refer to economies of spatial scope, commodity scope, or time scope, whenever the cost of producing the whole set is less than the sum of costs for the partition. Diseconomies of scope reflect the opposite. Within this context, the use of aggregates to describe transport output distorts the analysis of scale and reduces (and sometimes destroys) the possibility of analyzing scope. However, aggregation does provide a way to handle large number of variables, making it possible to estimate cost functions in practice. The question is, then, if we can use aggregates and yet find a way around their distorting nature. We will address this in what follows.

1.4.4. Marginal costs, elasticities and scale from aggregates

Whenever a cost function is specified in terms of one or more output aggregates, the analyst obtains a series of coefficients that can be given a microeconomic interpretation by simple association with properties like (1.21) or (1.23). If the function is a translog-around-the-mean, first order coefficients are 'output' elasticities, and the inverse of their sum could be offered as an estimate of the degree of scale economies. This is a procedure that has been frequently applied in the literature with some qualifications. Just as an example, Caves *et al.* (1980) included passenger-kilometers, ton-kilometers, average length of haul (freight) and average trip length (passengers) in their translog specification, and then calculated an estimate of the degree of scale economies, $\tilde{S}$, in various ways, always using the cost elasticities (obtained directly from the coefficients). Cost elasticities for ton and passenger-kilometers were always used, but the average-distance elasticities were left out in one of the measures of $\tilde{S}$ and included in other. The reason offered was that ton or passenger-kilometers might increase due to either more or longer trips. In fact, a coefficient of 0.5 on the elasticity of the average trip distance variables was suggested as a compromise. The thing is that an increase in the mean distance traveled necessarily requires that flows in the more distant O-D pairs have to increase more than flows in the relatively closer ones, and this violates the condition for scale analysis which relates to *proportional expansions* of output. Failure to look at S properly is in fact the main cause of ambiguity in this example; S is related with proportional expansions within the vector of flows Y, and not directly to changes in ton- or passenger-kilometers.

The fact that aggregates make the calculation of S obscure was highlighted by Gagné (1990) and by Ying (1992) who pointed out that aggregates are usually interrelated; for example ton-kilometers is equal to total flow times average length of haul, a fact that had not been taken into account when making calculations of S. It was not realized, however, that this arises because aggregates are a function of flows. This is a key observation that allows a rigorous analysis of the problem.

Let $\tilde{Y} \in \Re^n$ be the vector of aggregates with components $\tilde{y}_j$ (for example ton-kilometers, total flow, less-than-truckload movements, etc). Most of these $\tilde{y}_j$ are implicit constructs from the components of Y. This is evident in the case of ton-kilometers (equation (1.46)) or total flow (for example total passengers in a period) which is simply the summation over all y_i. Thus, if $\tilde{y}_j$ is an implicit function of Y, then an estimated $\tilde{C}(w, \tilde{Y})$ is an implicit representation $\hat{C}$ of $C(w, Y)$ because (Jara-Díaz and Cortés, 1996)

$$\tilde{C}(w, \tilde{Y}) \equiv \tilde{C}\left[w, \tilde{Y}(Y)\right] \equiv \hat{C}(w, Y) \tag{1.47}$$

Assume $\tilde{C}(w, \tilde{Y})$ is a good representation of the cost minimizing process, i.e. it is the best econometric effort to capture the cost structure. Therefore, although $C(Y)$ cannot be estimated directly, the microeconomic properties of $C(Y)$ can be recovered from $\tilde{C}(w, \tilde{Y})$. In particular, marginal costs with respect to the components y_i of Y can be obtained as (evaluated at any point)

$$\frac{\partial \hat{C}}{\partial y_i} = \sum_{j=1}^{n} \frac{\partial \tilde{C}}{\partial \tilde{y}_j} \frac{\partial \tilde{y}_j}{\partial y_i} \tag{1.48}$$

and the elasticity of cost with respect to y_i as

$$\hat{\eta}_i = \frac{\partial \hat{C}}{\partial y_i} \frac{y_i}{C} = \frac{y_i}{C} \sum_{j=1}^{n} \frac{\partial \tilde{C}}{\partial \tilde{y}_j} \frac{\partial \tilde{y}_j}{\partial y_i} \tag{1.49}$$

or

$$\hat{\eta}_i = \sum_{j=1}^{n} \frac{\partial \tilde{y}_j}{\partial y_i} \frac{y_i}{\tilde{y}_j} \frac{\partial \tilde{C}}{\partial \tilde{y}_j} \frac{\tilde{y}_j}{C} \tag{1.50}$$

that is,

$$\hat{\eta}_i = \sum_{j=1}^{n} \varepsilon_{ji} \tilde{\eta}_j \qquad (1.51)$$

where ε_{ji} is the elasticity of aggregate output $\tilde{y}_j$ with respect to y_i, and $\tilde{\eta}_j$ is the elasticity of $\tilde{C}$ with respect to $\tilde{y}_j$, i.e.

$$\varepsilon_{ji} = \frac{\partial \tilde{y}_j}{\partial y_i} \frac{y_i}{\tilde{y}_j} \qquad \text{and} \qquad \tilde{\eta}_j = \frac{\partial \tilde{C}}{\partial \tilde{y}_j} \frac{\tilde{y}_j}{C} \qquad (1.52)$$

Then the correct calculation of an estimate $\hat{S}$ for S can be obtained as

$$\hat{S} = \left[\sum_i \hat{\eta}_i \right]^{-1} = \left[\sum_j \alpha_j \tilde{\eta}_j \right]^{-1} \qquad (1.53)$$

where

$$\alpha_j = \sum_i \varepsilon_{ji} \qquad (1.54)$$

Note that each "aggregate elasticity" is weighted by a term, which is the (local) degree of homogeneity with respect to Y -calculated explicitly in equation (1.54)- that involves all elasticities of the corresponding aggregate output $\tilde{y}$ with respect to each disaggregate component y_i. In summary, the correct estimate is not necessarily equal to the inverse of the sum of the aggregate's elasticities, $\tilde{\eta}_j$, unless the α_j's are all equal to one.

The procedure to use $\tilde{C}$ correctly rests upon the relation between the $\tilde{y}_j$'s and the y_i's. But, according to equation (1.53), this applies to all arguments of $\tilde{C}$ which are functions of Y, no matter how they are called (i.e. characteristics, attributes or outputs). Thus, equation (1.54) provides a test for the inclusion of any aggregate elasticity in the calculation of $\hat{S}$. Just as an example, we show here the coefficients α_j which correspond to a ton-kilometers variable (*TK*) and an average length of haul variable (*ALH*).

Example 1.5
Consider the most popular output aggregate, ton-kilometers or pax-kilometers, *TK*. The explicit function and the weight of this component is very direct, that is,

$$TK = \sum_i y_i d_i \qquad (1.55)$$

$$\alpha_{TK} = \sum_i \varepsilon_{TKi} = \sum_i \frac{\partial TK}{\partial y_i} \frac{y_i}{TK} = \sum_i d_i \frac{y_i}{TK} = 1 \qquad (1.56)$$

where d_i, the distance traveled in O-D pair i, has been assumed to remain constant. This result tells us that $\tilde{\eta}_{TK}$ fully contributes to the calculation of $\hat{S}$, if TK is included in $\tilde{C}(\tilde{Y})$.

Let us move to the average length of haul, which is

$$ALH = \frac{\sum_i y_i d_i}{\sum_i y_i} \tag{1.57}$$

Its α_j corresponds to

$$\alpha_{ALH} = \sum_i \frac{\partial ALH}{\partial y_i} \frac{y_i}{ALH} = \sum_i \left[\frac{d_i \sum_r y_r - \sum_r y_r d_r}{\left(\sum_r y_r\right)^2} \right] \frac{y_i}{\sum_r y_r d_r} \sum_r y_r \tag{1.58}$$

$$\alpha_{ALH} = \sum_i \left[\frac{d_i y_i}{\sum_r y_r d_r} - \frac{y_i}{\sum_r y_r} \right] = 1 - 1 = 0 \tag{1.59}$$

In this case the conclusion is that the elasticity of *ALH* should not be used in the calculation of $\hat{S}$ whenever O-D distances remain constant after O-D flows grow by the same proportion. Note that distances might not remain constant if a proportional expansion of flows induces a variation in the route structure.

These are simple cases to illustrate how to proceed with a $\tilde{C}(w, \tilde{Y})$ function. A fairly complete analysis of nearly all forms of output description and their role in the calculation of $\hat{S}$ is contained in Jara-Díaz and Cortés (1996). It is relevant to note that the α_j's are not necessarily equal to either zero or one. Sometimes the value of the weight depends upon the particular manner in which each firm operates. Just to illustrate the point, consider the case of an output index that is in fact related with transport supply, like vehicle-kilometers. The relation between this index and the flow vector is dependent on the manner in which frequency and average load is adapted following an increase in the flows. It can be shown that a pure frequency adjustment makes $\alpha_j = 1$ and a pure load adjustment (which has a limit) makes $\alpha_j = 0$; most cases would be in between, making $0 \leq \alpha_j \leq 1$.

1.4.5. Economies of density and economies of network size

In transport, the use of aggregates -that normally obviates the spatial dimension of product- has provoked the need to make a distinction between economies of *scale* and economies of *density*, which have been associated to a varying or constant network size respectively. The usual approach is based upon an estimated cost function $\tilde{C}(\tilde{Y};N)$ where $\tilde{Y}$ is a vector of aggregated product descriptions (including the so-called attributes) and N is a variable representing the network (factor prices are suppressed for simplicity). Returns to density (RTD) and returns to scale (RTS) (Caves, Christensen and Swanson, 1981) are defined as

$$RTD = \frac{1}{\sum_{j \in J} \tilde{\eta}_j} \tag{1.60}$$

$$RTS = \frac{1}{\sum_{j \in J} \tilde{\eta}_j + \eta_N} \tag{1.61}$$

where $\tilde{\eta}_j$ is the elasticity of $\tilde{C}(\tilde{Y};N)$ with respect to aggregate product j and η_N is the elasticity with respect to N. J is the subset of aggregates considered in the calculation (my notation), which varies from study to study. They fulfill $RTS < RTD$ since the network elasticity is positive (as obtained in all empirical studies). RTD assumes a constant network when output increases (increase in density), while RTS assumes that the network grows as well (increase in output through a network expansion) but keeping density constant.

Increasing returns to scale ($RTS > 1$) suggest that both product and network size should be increased because serving larger networks would diminish average cost. Constant returns to scale together with increasing returns to density ($RTD > 1$) would indicate that traffic should be increased keeping network constant. This apparently straightforward analysis has nevertheless an evident limitation: as $RTS < RTD$ a firm that has both optimal density and optimal network size cannot be described. Moreover, if network size was optimal ($RTS = 1$) the firm *must* exhibit increasing returns to density.

Most empirical studies of the airline industry (where the number of points served, PS, is the usual network variable), have reported the presence of increasing returns to density and constant returns to scale, as concluded by Caves, Christensen and Tretheway (1984), Kirby (1986), Gillen, Oum and Tretheway (1985, 1990), Oum and Zhang (1991), Kumbhakar (1992), Keeler and Formby (1994) and Baltagi, Griffin and Rich (1995), among others. These results indicate that, on costs grounds, it would be advantageous for firms to increase traffic densities on their networks, but it would be inconvenient to expand their networks. Observed industry behavior, however, was different: after deregulation –in the U.S. first and then in the rest of the world– the air industry has concentrated and the networks served have expanded through mergers, alliances and acquisitions. Thus, firms have tried to increase their network size, which seems to contradict constant returns to scale as previously defined. Two reactions emerged; on one hand, some authors have argued that network growth can be understood as an attempt to exploit economies of traffic density (e.g. Oum and Tretheway, 1990; Brueckner and Spiller, 1994). On the other hand, a series of re-examinations of the methods to calculate scale economies for all transport industries have been proposed in the literature (Gagné, 1990; Ying 1992; Xu et al., 1994; Oum and Zhang, 1997).

The method for the correct calculation of economies of scale from aggregates presented in section 1.4.4 shows that, in a rigorous sense, it yields an improved version of what today is understood as economies of density in the transport economics literature, because network variations (changes in N) are not allowed. Scale in terms of the true product Y –from now on referred as *disaggregated scale*– is in fact *density* in terms of $\widetilde{Y}$. It should be added, though, that economies of density (*RTD*) is defined in the literature under the condition of an invariant route structure. As pointed out earlier in Example 1.5, this needs not be the case when a proportional expansion of true product induces a variation in the optimal route structure. Therefore, **it is better to keep referring to *RTD* when the correct calculation is done assuming that routes do not vary, and to multiproduct scale economies *S* when routes are allow to be readjusted** The main practical implication is that the calculation of the α weights in S should account for the variation of distances with flows. Of course, when the optimal adjustment to a proportional increase in flows does not require a change in route structure, both concepts coincide. Note also that the method presented in section 1.4.4 makes it unnecessary to define the J set a priori as all aggregates should be taken into account and the α's will take care of the importance of each one in the calculation of S.

What about *RTS*, the relevant index when analyzing network growth? In this direction, by looking at $\widetilde{Y}$ in terms of Y, *economies of scale with variable network size, RTS (scale* in terms of $\widetilde{Y}$ and N) have been shown to be inadequate to study the costs effects of network expansions (Basso and Jara-Díaz, 2006). In essence, this happens because *RTS* imposes that the traffic density –roughly the average load per link– remains constant after the network expansion, a condition that looks reasonable when considering $\widetilde{Y}$ but has been shown to impose quite unreasonable relations among flows when considering Y. Then, we know how to detect the presence of economies of density/disaggregate scale, but we do not have a method to analyze the cost convenience of network expansions (or reductions) from cost functions estimated in terms of aggregated products. A new method, that replaces *RTS* in this task, is needed.

Increasing network size is unambiguously associated with an increase in the number of products and, therefore, networks variables are related with economies of scope. Consequently, the correct approach is the calculation of economies of spatial scope (Basso and Jara-Díaz, 2005). This is particularly evident when N is represented by the number of points served, *PS*, because increasing *PS* implies increasing the number of O-D flows. Note also that learning the extent of economies of scope is of interest not only to assess the cost convenience of network expansions, but also because economies of scope and scale are related with subadditivity, that is, with the existence of natural monopoly.

1.4.6. Spatial scope from aggregates

Here we present an approach to calculate spatial scope from transport cost functions with aggregate output, also resting on the relation $\widetilde{y}_h \equiv \widetilde{y}_h(Y)$. But, just as behind *RTS* lays a constant density imposition in order to control for the value of aggregated flows after a network expansion, this method to calculate scope will impose a related condition on the disaggregated flows. It not only allows to study the cost convenience (or inconvenience) of network growth, but also provides a way of incorporating the density explanation in a strict economic way by considering cost changes produced by both density and network size increases.

The degree of economies of scope (*SC*) in a spatial sense deals with costs when O-D pairs are added. Thus, within the context of variable networks, *spatial scope* is useful to analyze whether a certain firm serving PS^A nodes with $PS^A \cdot (PS^A - 1)$ potential O-D flows should expand its network to serve PS^C nodes, adding $PS^C \cdot (PS^C - 1) - PS^A \cdot (PS^A - 1)$ new flows, or whether these new flows should be served by a new firm (which would deal with PS^B nodes). To be precise through an example, see Figure 1.10, where a firm serves two O-D pairs (scenario A). *SC* can be used to analyze the convenience of adding four new O-D pairs through the addition of the new node 3 (i.e. adopting scenario C). This analysis can be done using the three vectors $Y^A = \{y_{12}, y_{21}, 0, 0, 0, 0\}$, $Y^B = \{0, 0, y_{13}, y_{31}, y_{23}, y_{32}\}$ and $Y^C = \{y_{12}, y_{21}, y_{13}, y_{31}, y_{23}, y_{32}\}$. A positive value for *SC* would indicate incentives to add node 3, producing vector Y^C. Note the incremental cost of serving a new node is given by $C(Y^C) - C(Y^A)$, which will be different from $C(Y^B)$ unless *SC* is nil[5].

Let us analyze the general case of network expansion. Even if the true (disaggregated) product vectors Y^A, Y^B and Y^C were unknown, *SC* could still be calculated correctly if the corresponding aggregates $\tilde{Y}(Y^A)$, $\tilde{Y}(Y^B)$ and $\tilde{Y}(Y^D)$ were known, and an estimated cost function $\tilde{C}(\tilde{Y}, PS)$ was available (Jara-Díaz, Cortés and Ponce, 2001). Analytically, *SC* could be calculated through

$$SC^A = SC^B = \frac{\tilde{C}\left(\tilde{Y}(Y^A), PS^A\right) + \tilde{C}\left(\tilde{Y}(Y^B), PS^B\right) - \tilde{C}\left(\tilde{Y}(Y^C), PS^C\right)}{\tilde{C}\left(\tilde{Y}(Y^C), PS^C\right)} \qquad (1.62)$$

where $PS^C = PS^B > PS^A$ (as in the example of Figure 1.10). Note the arguments of $\tilde{C}(\tilde{Y}, PS)$ in equation (1.62) are not evaluated at zero output levels, unlike $C(\cdot)$ in equation (1.24), allowing the use of translog cost functions directly for the calculation of scope[6]. This happens because the aggregate representations (like total passengers or ton-kilometers) do not vanish when some of the O-D flows go to zero as in Y^A or Y^B.

In the absence of more information, some reasonable condition has to be imposed regarding the magnitude of the flows added after the network expansion, in order to assign values to the aggregates in both $\tilde{Y}^B$ and $\tilde{Y}^C$, given that one knows $(\tilde{Y}^A; PS^A)$. This type of requirement is not new; the condition behind the calculation of *RTS* is *density does not change*, but this is imposed on the aggregates, not on the true flow vector *Y*, inducing

---

[5] For the graphical representation of the *n*-nodes case see Jara-Diaz *et al.* (2001).
[6] Of course one has to maintain the assumption that the estimated cost function does a good job in describing costs, in spite of being specified with aggregate descriptions of product. In other words, $\tilde{C}(\tilde{Y}) \equiv \tilde{C}\left(\tilde{Y}(Y)\right) \equiv \hat{C}(Y)$

unreasonable analytical restrictions on the new O-D flows (i.e. those behind Y^B). If a condition is needed in order to asses the impacts of a network expansion on costs, it should be imposed on the true product, the flow vector Y, even if one is working with aggregates for econometric purposes. This will allow consistent and more reasonable inferences later on. **This method proposes to calculate economies of spatial scope using equation (1.62), under the condition that the average O-D flow of each cargo type remains constant after the network expansion.** Formally, we define the average origin-destination flow for cargo type k as

$$ AOD_k = \frac{\sum_i \sum_j y_{ijk}}{NOD} \tag{1.63} $$

where y_{ijk} represents the flow of type k between origin i and destination j and NOD is the total number of O-D pairs served. Note the numerator in equation (1.63) is total tons T if k indicates freight and total passengers P if k refers to persons. This means the two indices ought to be calculated if in the study in question freight and passenger services are provided. Holding this index (indices) constant when calculating economies of spatial scope through equation (1.63) will help the analytical estimation of the values of the components of both $\widetilde{Y}^B$ and $\widetilde{Y}^C$. The idea is simple: calculate AOD_k^A from $(\widetilde{Y}^A; PS^A)$, and then estimate $\widetilde{Y}^C$ and $\widetilde{Y}^B$ with the help of $AOD_k^C \equiv AOD_k^A$.

Some of the new O-D flows –which will be in average as large as the originals- will circulate in the original portion of the network, increasing density, provided they are not all directly served. This will be cost convenient if increasing returns to density are present. But, by calculating SC, the costs of the network expansion itself will be properly captured this time, as is evident from equation (1.62). It is not surprising that increasing returns to density favors the presence of economies of spatial scope even though they represent totally different ways of increasing output. After all, economies of density represent economies of scale in terms of the true product Y and is well-know that the presence of economies of scope favors economies of scale and vice versa because of a general theoretical property (equation (1.28)). It must be clear, however, that even in the presence of decreasing or constant returns to density/disaggregated scale, economies of spatial scope may exist (Jara-Díaz and Basso, 2003)[7]. Finally, note that a proportional expansion of all flows in all O-D pairs (which is what lies behind the strict notion of scale), makes AOD and density (as understood in the literature) grow by the same proportion. Therefore, the relation between density and disaggregated scale remains intact with the proposed approach.

---

[7] This could happen because of the same alleged reasons why there might be increasing RTS, as for example shared use of airport and ground personnel, handling baggage transfers and passengers check-in (see for example Oum Park and Zhang, 2000). Recall, however, that $SC>0$ and $RTD=1$ cannot be paralleled by $RTS>1$ and $RTD=1$ since $RTS<RTD$ analytically (Basso and Jara-Diaz, 2003).

Example 1.6

Let us illustrate this general approach with a specific –although popular– example. Let us consider an aggregated cost function $\tilde{C}(TK, ALH, PS)$ where TK represents ton-kilometers and ALH represents average length of haul, as defined in equations (1.55) and (1.57). We would like to examine whether a certain firm with cost given by $\tilde{C}(TK^A, ALH^A, PS^A)$, has cost incentives to connect new nodes (e.g. airports) assuming that the new O-D flows have, in average, the same magnitudes as those already served (constant *AOD*), or if it is better to have another firm serving them. The expanded network will have a size given by PS^C, the incremental cost of serving the new flows is given by $\tilde{C}(TK^C, ALH^C, PS^C) - \tilde{C}(TK^A, ALH^A, PS^A)$, and the cost of producing these new flows with a different firm is $\tilde{C}(TK^B, ALH^B, PS^B)$. Then, replacing terms in (1.62), what should be calculated is

$$SC^A = \frac{\tilde{C}(TK^A, ALH^A, PS^A) + \tilde{C}(TK^B, ALH^B, PS^B) - \tilde{C}(TK^C, ALH^C, PS^C)}{\tilde{C}(TK^C, ALH^C, PS^C)} \tag{1.64}$$

In (1.64), we only know TK^A, ALH^A and PS^A, which represents the point where economies of spatial scope will be calculated. The value of PS^C will depend on the size of the network increase that we would like to study, e.g. one or five nodes. As RTS is a local marginal measure, it is reasonable to consider a marginal change in network size, i.e. one node, which implies $PS^C = PS^A + 1$. From this case, every network expansion can be analyzed incrementally. We will assume that the firm in scenarios A and C potentially serve all corresponding O-D pairs, which means

$$NOD^A = PS^A \cdot (PS^A - 1) \tag{1.65}$$

$$NOD^C = PS^C \cdot (PS^C - 1) = PS^A \cdot (PS^A + 1) \tag{1.66}$$

The average O-D flow before the expansion is given by

$$AOD^A = \frac{T^A}{NOD^A} \tag{1.67}$$

where T^A is total tons moved by the firm, i.e. $T^A = \sum_{ij} y_{ij}^A$. As *ALH* is the ratio between *TK* and *T*, equation (1.67) can be re-written as

$$AOD^A = \frac{TK^A}{ALH^A \cdot NOD^A} \tag{1.68}$$

After the network expansion, the average O-D flow is given by

$$AOD^C = \frac{TK^C}{ALH^C \cdot NOD^C} \qquad (1.69)$$

Using the constant AOD condition, which implies equality between (1.68) and (1.69), and replacing equations (1.65) and (1.66), we get

$$TK^C = TK^A \cdot \frac{ALH^C}{ALH^A} \cdot \frac{PS^A + 1}{PS^A - 1} \qquad (1.70)$$

Equation (1.70) shows that assigning a value to TK^C requires an estimate of the (potential) variation of the average length of haul after the addition of one node to the network, ALH^C.

Next, we need estimates for TK^B and ALH^B. The former can be estimated as

$$TK^B = \sum_{ij} y_{ij}^B \cdot d_{ij} = \sum_{ij} y_{ij}^C \cdot d_{ij} - \sum_{ij} y_{ij}^A \cdot d_{ij} = TK^C - TK^A \qquad (1.71)$$

This implies distances traveled by the original flows (scenario A) do not vary after the new node is added. As the route structure is an endogenous firm decision, distances could change if the route structure is changed. In this case some empirical relation has to be found. Two things should be noted. First, assuming distances traveled by the original flows do not change ensures that, after the network expansion, the incorporation of the new flows will increase the density on the original portion of the network, as long as the new O-D pairs are not served exclusively by direct services. Second, ALH may still change because the new flows do not need to travel, in average, the same distances as the original flows. On the other hand, the equality $T^B = T^C - T^A$ stands without discussion.

Once TK^B has been calculated, the respective average length of haul can be obtained from

$$ALH^B = \frac{TK^B}{T^B} = \frac{TK^B}{T^C - T^A} \Rightarrow ALH^B = \frac{TK^B}{\dfrac{TK^C}{ALH^C} - \dfrac{TK^A}{ALH^A}} \qquad (1.72)$$

Note that equation (1.72) for ALH^B is valid in general, irrespective of the alternative chosen to estimate ALH^C. In particular, if $ALH^C = ALH^A$, then $ALH^B = ALH^A$. Finally, plugging the estimated values in equation (1.64) using the available cost function yields an estimate for the degree of spatial scope economies.

Evidently, a different set of aggregated products in the cost function would require other sequence and specific calculations, e.g. the use of passenger-kilometers mean that PK^C and PK^B should be calculated from PK^A taking into account average length of trip instead of average length of haul. Although a case by case analysis is necessary for other aggregates and attributes, the key aspect is to study analytically the behavior of each one under the constant average O-D flow condition.

The degree of economies of spatial scope calculated with the method proposed above has a main objective: to investigate whether there are cost advantages for the firms to expand their network size. This, in conjunction with the degree of economies of density/disaggregated scale, will allow a correct analysis of the industry structure taking into account both density (level of production) and network size.

1.5. Synthesis

The theory of transport production involves two key aspects: transport output, which is a vector of flows with several dimensions, and operating rules, i.e. the forms of input combinations to produce a flow vector. The main elements here are frequency, load size, route structure, and so on, which are operating decisions. On the other hand, fleet size, vehicle capacity, loading-unloading capacity, rights-of-way design, and so on are decisions related with input acquisition. Both types of decisions are related, but the former is taken within the boundaries of the latter. In this chapter we have emphasized that it is the spatial dimension of product what distinguishes transport production from other industries.

A given network and set of O-D flows can be served in different ways, and using simple networks we have given examples of such service structures as cyclical systems and hub-and-spoke, showing how key variables like fleet size change from one case to another, and how these results depend both on flow levels and network topology. For known input prices, the firm can find the optimal combination of inputs and operating rules for any service and route structure –the actual sequence of links followed by vehicles on the network– which is a discrete decision. This yields conditional cost functions, such that the transport cost function corresponds to the minimum among these.

The important concepts of economies of scale and scope, which represent the behavior of costs under different forms of product expansion, have been presented here paying attention to their rigorous definitions, that is, explicitly considering the multiproduct nature of transport production and accordingly using the (true) vector of products in the calculations. Scale relates with proportional expansions of flows and scope deals with orthogonal partitions of those flows, which originates particular types of scope analysis; spatial scope deals with the relevant issue of network size and shape.

But estimating scale and scope requires information about costs. In most cases, however, transport operations are too complex to be represented by detailed and direct relations between vehicles, travel times, loading/unloading times, etc, their prices and product, so we use estimated cost functions to understand these dependencies in a more abstract fashion. Despite being "black-boxes", estimated cost functions are a necessary tool to synthetically represent the behavior of costs with respect to input prices and the flow vector.

Estimating cost functions in transport has a problem of its own, namely, the large number of products and, consequently, of parameters involved in any meaningful flexible econometric specification. It has become customary to represent output through aggregate variables in an effort to reduce these requirements, thus generating functions expressed in terms of passenger-kilometers and such. Although this strategy has proven to be successful for estimation purposes, answers to important questions such as the value of marginal costs, degree of scale economies and degree of scope economies, have become obscure. The old problem of loosing information due to aggregation, take us in this matter to misleading results. Fortunately, the aggregation problem can be worked around if one considers the specific formulation used to compute each aggregation, i.e., making explicit that costs really depend on the disaggregate variables, or in other words, recognizing aggregates are only an estimation device that should not change the true essence of the problem.

Under the general discussion of aggregation and how to deal with it, the chapter paid special attention to Returns to Density (*RTD*) and Returns to Scale (*RTS*), two indices aimed at analyzing cost behavior under (aggregated) output expansions. Both have important problems of interpretation due to the ambiguity generated through aggregation. By expressing aggregates as a function of true output, we have shown that *RTD* –defined over a given transport network- corresponds to a limited form of scale in a strict sense. On the other hand, the potential advantages of expanding the served network has been analyzed in the literature by means of the *RTS* index, a scale-like construct that imposes flows and network to grow by the same proportion holding density constant, which has been shown to hide implicit inadequate relations among flows. This prevents a meaningful industry structure analysis regarding optimal network size, which requires the calculation of spatial scope instead. We have presented a method to do it.

We have shown here that network expansions can be properly analyzed by looking at the true product and its translation into a vector of aggregates. This viewpoint has originated both the method to calculate spatial scope and the approach to calculate returns to density/scale correctly. This implies that a fairly complete and meaningful analysis of a transport industry structure can be performed from aggregated transport cost functions provided they are correctly interpreted.

Appendix: Calculation of the multiproduct degree of Scale Economies from a cost function.

If

$$F(X,Y) = 0 \tag{A.1}$$

defines optimal production of Y from X, then

$$C(w,Y) = \sum_i w_i \cdot x_i \tag{A.2}$$

On the other hand, S is defined by

$$F(\lambda X, \lambda^S Y) = 0 \tag{A.3}$$

This means that

$$C(w, \lambda^S Y) = \sum_i w_i \cdot \lambda x_i \tag{A.4}$$

Combining (A.2) and (A.4)

$$C(w, \lambda^S Y) \equiv \lambda \cdot C(w,Y) \tag{A.5}$$

Deriving both sides of (A.5) with respect to y_i

$$\frac{\partial C}{\partial (\lambda^S y_i)} \lambda^S \equiv \lambda \frac{\partial C}{\partial y_i} \tag{A.6}$$

Deriving both sides of (A.5) with respect to λ

$$\sum_i \frac{\partial C}{\partial (\lambda^S y_i)} S\lambda^{S-1} y_i \equiv C(w,Y) \tag{A.7}$$

Replacing (A.6) into (A.7)

$$\sum_i S \frac{\partial C}{\partial y_i} y_i \equiv C(w,Y) \tag{A.8}$$

$$S = \frac{C(w,Y)}{\sum_i \dfrac{\partial C}{\partial y_i} y_i} \tag{A.9}$$

2. Travel Demand and Value of Time

2.1. Introduction

When estimating travel demand, we may approach each individual's decision-process as if it consisted of three parts: whether to travel at all, where and when to travel, and by what means. In practice, these give rise to the three classical transport model types, namely, generation, distribution and mode choice. What is noteworthy is that regardless of the specific functions one can propose for such modeling, it is common to all that time is assumed to be a very valuable resource; one which consumption individuals would be happy to diminish. In other words, models have to reflect the fact that individuals would rather be doing something else, either at home, at work, or somewhere else, than riding a bus or driving a car.

The value of time, then, is paramount in transport modeling and is certainly behind the demand function we use, either explicitly or implicitly. Accordingly, it should come as no surprise that a rather important amount of effort in transport economics is devoted to determine this *willingness to pay to reduce travel time* underlying people's decision processes. Viability of transport projects and services depend on it.

Even though generation and distribution models may help estimating the value of time, it has become customary to use modal choice models for that purpose. With these popular models, such estimation is quite straightforwardly computed as the ratio of two parameters, an operation that is now common practice. However, mode choice models are just a specific form of modeling demand -people facing discrete choices-, and consequently we can, an we will in this chapter, explore the subject of discrete choice within the general framework of consumer' behavior and utility maximization, and by doing so gain more insight into the formulation and interpretation of the results obtained from those model types.

But we will go further than that. If we widen our perspective, it should be easy to see that a person's problem of making a transport decision is actually a sub problem of the general issue of assigning time to activities. Working, spending time with friends, shopping, reading a book and commuting are all things that have to be carried out within a very fixed and restrictive time frame of twenty-four hours, so what people really do is organize their time according to preferences and restrictions. By fully understanding this process, the more precise nature of the value of time should emerge, so that should be our true goal. Understanding travel demand may indeed be as understanding life itself.

2.2. Discrete choices in travel demand

2.2.1. General approach

One of the most common choices regarding travel at an individual level is that of mode choice in the morning trip to work or study. In Figure 2.1, four hypothetical alternatives for such a trip are represented, each one characterized by its cost C_i (price) and travel time from origin to destination, t_i. Mode 1 is the fastest and most expensive and mode 4 is the slowest but cheapest. If the individual is observed to choose alternative 2, *and nothing else mattered,* it means that he or she is not willing to pay an extra amount C_1-C_2 to save t_2-t_1 time units. On the other hand, such choice implies a willingness to pay of C_2-C_3 to save t_3-t_2 time units. For short, that person "values" travel time more than $(C_2-C_3)/(t_3-t_2)$ but less than $(C_1-C_2)/(t_2-t_1)$.

It can be shown that the above can be interpreted as the result of an individual choice commanded by the maximization of a utility function that values positively available time $\tau-t_i$ and available money $I-C_i$, where τ is the period considered and I is personal income. This way, by choosing among modes the individual is trading time for purchasing power. To see this, consider a linear version of such a function, $\alpha(\tau-t_i) + \beta(I-C_i)$ which maximization in Figure 2.1 is equivalent to the minimization of $\alpha\,t_i+\beta\,C_i$. The three lines U_A, U_B and U_C represent three utility levels such that utility increases towards the origin where t_i and C_i are minimized (or $\tau-t_i$ and $I-C_i$ are maximized). This would yield to alternative 2 if the slope α/β is in the range between $(C_1-C_2)/(t_2-t_1)$ and $(C_2-C_3)/(t_3-t_2)$. This is the simplest view of a discrete travel choice process, but it helps understanding why discrete choice models are the most popular type of travel demand models. Note that α/β is measured in monetary units per unit time.

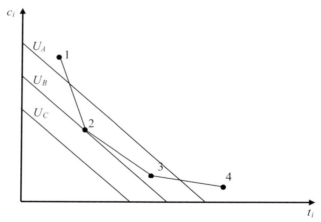

Figure 2.1. *Simple mode choice as utility maximization*

Choices between fast but expensive modes and slow but cheap ones are of usual occurrence not only in daily travel but in most occasions. For example, going from an airport to the city usually has three or four types of alternatives: a scheduled bus part of the urban system (as in Oslo and Buenos Aires), an express bus service (as the OrlyBus in Paris), a door-to-door share minibus (as in Santiago, Chile) and taxicabs, listed from the cheapest to the most expensive.

Expanding on this simple view, in discrete choice models the individual chooses among several alternatives, which differ in cost and characteristics. The most important element in this approach is the formulation of a (alternative-specific) utility function, usually represented through a linear combination of cost and characteristics of each alternative, also including socio-economic variables for each group of individuals. This constitutes the deterministic part of utility, to which a random component is added; it is the probabilistic properties of such random term that generate the various models used in practice. In this Chapter, and in this book indeed, we will deal only with the deterministic part such that whenever we use the word utility we will be referring to the variables, form and properties of the non-random utility associated to each discrete alternative. Note the deterministic part alone poses several questions regarding model specification: functional form of the observable part, type and form of variables that should be used, and criteria to decide which group of individuals will be regarded as "alike".

The choice of the word "utility" to describe the equation that represents the level of satisfaction associated to each alternative is not casual. It is borrowed from the terminology in microeconomics, which provides the foundations to understand the role of income, time, characteristics, preferences, etc. exposed in the next section. Two caveats should be made. First, the primary sources of utility will not be examined (i.e. the psychological mechanisms that make consumption or actions pleasurable). Secondly, and in order to avoid confusion, it is important to stress that what is typically called utility to describe an alternative in discrete choice models, is really a *conditional indirect utility function* that already includes other constraints faced by the individual (see Definition 2.1 below).

2.2.2. The discrete choice framework: quality and income

The traditional microeconomic framework for consumer's behavior is stated in terms of a bundle of continuous-in-nature goods X that are chosen by the individual in an attempt to obtain the maximum level of satisfaction $U(X)$, within all possible bundles allowed by his/her purchasing power. After the formalization of Lancaster (1966), who introduced the notion of goods characteristics as the primary source of utility, the level of satisfaction could be stated in terms of those characteristics (flavor, nutrient, warmth, beauty); accordingly, the problem of choice can be understood properly accounting for the fact that characteristics can be obtained through the purchase of market goods, which in turn require money.

There is a relevant type of consumer's decision which can be modeled with a slight modification of the preceding framework: discrete choices. Such a problem arises when the decision to acquire one unit of a certain generic good (e.g. a car, fruit or a trip) is followed by the choice of a specific type (e.g. a car model, a fruit type, a transport mode). Then the consumer can be viewed as choosing both the amount of continuous goods and one of the discrete alternatives (mode), each one described by a vector Q_j containing its qualitative characteristics q_{kj}, which directly affect utility. Formally (adapting from McFadden, 1981), an individual is assumed to behave as follows:

$$\underset{X,j}{Max}U(X,Q_j) \tag{2.1}$$

$$\sum_i P_i X_i + c_j \leq I \tag{2.2}$$

$$j \in M$$

where U is utility, P_i and X_i are the price and quantity of good i respectively, c_j is the cost of acquiring discrete alternative j, I is money income and M is the set of discrete alternatives.

As the choice of j is discrete and of X is continuous, the problem can be seen as having two steps:
-   First, find the optimal consumption X conditional on the discrete choice j, which is a traditional consumer behavior problem with income given by $I - c_j$, generating conditional demands $X_i(P, I - c_j, Q_j)$.
-   Second, optimize over j, which is a discrete choice, obtaining the overall maximum.

Definition 2.1: Conditional indirect utility function
The conditional indirect utility function V_j represents the maximum utility the individual would reach if alternative j was chosen.

As the first step yields conditional demands $X_i(P, I - c_j, Q_j)$, then $V_j \equiv U[X(P, I - c_j, Q_j), Q_j]$. Then the chosen alternative can be interpreted as that which fulfills $V_j > V_i \forall i \neq j$, such that the unconditional utility function V is the maximum V_j. Note that this means that not necessarily all arguments in V_j will actually influence the discrete choice. We will call the portion of V_j that decides the result of the discrete comparison a **truncated conditional indirect utility**, $\overline{U}_j$; also note that the truncation might come from the cancellation of either additive or multiplicative terms, or from both (see Example 2.1 below).

Definition 2.2: Marginal utility of income
The marginal utility of income is the variation (increase) in utility after an increase in income:

$$MUI = \frac{\partial V}{\partial I} \tag{2.3}$$

From Definition 2.1 and Definition 2.2 two properties follow:

-   $MUI = \dfrac{\partial V}{\partial I} = -\dfrac{\partial V_j}{\partial c_j}$
-   The so-called modal utility in discrete travel choice models is in fact a truncated conditional indirect utility function.

Definition 2.3: Subjective value of a characteristic
The subjective value of alternative j's characteristic k is the rate of substitution between quality and money at constant utility, and represents the willingness to pay to increase that quality in one unit, i.e.

$$SV_{kj} = \frac{\partial V / \partial q_{kj}}{\partial V / \partial I} \tag{2.4}$$

Note travel time is also a mode's quality, so we can define a **Subjective Value of Travel Time Savings (SVTTS)** in this same way. Note, however, that increasing quality means reducing transport time. We will return to this later.

Example 2.1
To illustrate the concept of truncated conditional indirect utility, let us represent V_j with a linear function, i.e.

$$V_j = \alpha + \sum_i \beta_i P_i + \sum_k \gamma_k q_{kj} + \lambda (I - c_j) \tag{2.5}$$

Which one is the largest value for V_j among all $j \in M$, will depend only on the characteristics in Q_j and the cost c_j (all other terms cancel out when comparing V_i and V_j). Thus, the relevant part of V_j for discrete choice modeling is

$$\overline{U}_j = -\lambda c_j + \sum_k \gamma_k q_{kj} \tag{2.6}$$

Equation (2.6) justifies the usual linear in cost and time (and other variables) specification of modal utility, so frequent in discrete travel choice models. According to equation (2.3), *MUI* is minus the coefficient of modal cost, λ, and SV_{kj} is simply the ratio of the corresponding quality coefficient over *MUI*, γ_k / λ. The attractive simplicity of this specification, though, is linked with an important limitation, as income vanishes from utility and therefore plays no role in travel behavior modeling. This is the case in McFadden's (1981) AIRUM model structure (Additive Income Random Utility Maximizing), which yields choice probabilities that are independent of current income. When the cost of the discrete good analyzed is small relative to income, such simplification is acceptable, but otherwise we would be ignoring the key role of income level in people's decision-making, which is actually the case for transport among many socioeconomic groups, particularly in developing nations.

A very simple extension of the usual linear utility model allows a much better understanding of the role of income (Jara-Díaz and Videla, 1989). For simplicity only, assume that the utility function U in (2.1) is separable in X and Q_j. This implies that the level of satisfaction attained from consuming a bundle X is independent of modal characteristics, i.e.

$$\frac{\partial^2 U}{\partial x_i \partial q_{jk}} = 0, \forall i, \forall j, k. \tag{2.7}$$

Under the separability assumption, we can write the utility function as

$$U\{X, Q_j\} = U_1(X) + U_2(Q_j) \tag{2.8}$$

The optimization problem on X has a solution that is conditional on c_j alone, yielding a set of functions $X^*(P, I - c_j)$; once they are replaced in $U_1(X)$, a partial indirect utility function is obtained, i.e.

$$\underset{X,j}{Max}[U_1(X)/\ PX^T \le I - c_j] \equiv V_1(P, I - c_j) \tag{2.9}$$

Thus the conditional indirect utility function is in fact

$$V(P, I - c_j, Q_j) = V_1(P, I - c_j) + U_2(Q_j) \tag{2.10}$$

The role of income involves V_1 only. Assuming that prices of continuous goods are constant, V_1 can be approximated by a Taylor expansion around (P, I), i.e.

$$V_1(P, I - c_j) = V_1(P, I) + \sum_{i=1}^{n} \frac{1}{i!} V_1^i(P, I)(-c_j)^i + R_{n+1} \tag{2.11}$$

where V_1^i denotes the i-th derivative of V_1 with respect to $I - c_j$ evaluated at I, and R_{n+1} represents terms of order $n+1$ and higher. If a Taylor expansion to the order n is assumed to be sufficiently accurate, then R_{n+1} is close to zero; therefore, V_1^n is a function of P only.

Then, V_j is given by

$$V_j = V_1(P, I) + \sum_{i=1}^{n-1} \frac{1}{i!} V_1^i(P, I)(-c_j)^i + \frac{1}{n!} V_1^n(P)(-c_j)^n + U_2(Q_j) \tag{2.12}$$

This shows that mode choice does depend on the level of individual income for $n \ge 2$, since at least one term of the form $V_1^i(P, I)$ will appear. This means that comparing $V(c_i, Q_i)$ against $V(c_j, Q_j)$ may yield a different result for different levels of income. In other words, if the best specification for V_j involves terms in c_j of order two or higher, then income influences mode choice.

From equation (2.12), the *MUI* can be calculated at an individual level as

$$\lambda = \frac{\partial V^*}{\partial I} = V_1^1(P, I) + \sum_{i=1}^{n-1} \frac{1}{i!} V_1^{i+1}(P, I)(-c_d)^i \tag{2.13}$$

where d stands for the chosen mode.

Example 2.2

This framework has been applied to a middle-low income corridor in Santiago, Chile (Jara-Díaz and Videla, 1989). Modal utility was specified using linear and squared terms in cost for the whole sample; as the squared term came out significant, the sample was divided into four homogeneous income groups and mode choice models were estimated using the second order specification. Within each sub-sample, the squared cost term came significant only for the three poorest groups, and its level diminished with income, which meant that the influence of income on choice decreased as purchasing power increased. Equation (2.13) was then applied to calculate the *MUI*, which was found to diminish with income, as expected. Other applications can be found in Ortúzar and González (2002).

2.2.3. The goods/leisure framework

The preceding approach to model discrete choices is fairly general, i.e. it applies to most type of purchasing decisions when the choice has to be made among a family of goods with qualitative internal differences. The transport-specific dimensions enter the picture when variables like the components of travel time (in-vehicle, waiting and access times) are included in Q_j (with a minus sign, as quality is defined as a positive aspect). An obvious alternative for modeling an activity like travel, in which the assignment of time is the basic dimension, is to include time in the framework from the beginning.

The analysis of travel choices within the framework of consumer behavior explicitly including time was a rather natural extension of the early theoretical attempts to account for time as a "requisite" for goods consumption (reviewed in the next section). By 1970, Gronau adapted Becker's (1965) theory to model mode choice including both time and money constraints, showing that the (discrete) decision depended on something that now we would call modal utility, which was a weighted sum of cost and travel time (see Gronau, 1986).

One of the most popular microeconomic approaches specifically aimed at understanding mode choice, is the goods/leisure trade-off framework (Train and McFadden, 1978), where modal travel time t_i and cost c_i are included as variables that influence utility through the impact on goods consumption G and leisure time L. This can be summarized as follows, for the case of a single trip in a given O-D pair:

$$\text{Max } U(G,L) \tag{2.14}$$

subject to

$$G + c_i = wW + E \tag{2.15}$$

$$L + W + t_i = \tau \tag{2.16}$$

$$i \in M$$

where
W is working time
w is wage rate
E is income from other sources
τ is total available time.

By virtue of equations (2.15) and (2.16), working more (increasing W) means consuming more (larger G) and reducing leisure time (lower L), and vice versa. Thus, the trade-off between goods and leisure -the only two possible sources of wellbeing in this formulation- is synthesized by W.

As in the previous problem, represented by equations (2.1) and (2.2), this one can be solved in two steps, using W as a "pivot", replacing G and L as functions of W from (2.15) and (2.16) in (2.14). Then the optimal value for W can be found conditional on mode choice (i.e. on c_i and t_i), which yields a conditional demand for working time W^* as a function of w, $E-c_i$ and $\tau - t_i$, that is,

$$\text{Max}\, U(G,L) = \text{Max}\, U(E - c_i - wW, \tau - t_i - W) \tag{2.17}$$

The optimal condition is

$$\frac{\partial U}{\partial W} = \frac{\partial U}{\partial G}\frac{\partial G}{\partial W} + \frac{\partial U}{\partial L}\frac{\partial L}{\partial W} = \frac{\partial U}{\partial G}w - \frac{\partial U}{\partial L} = 0 \tag{2.18}$$

$$\Rightarrow W^*(E - c_i, w, \tau - t_i) = W^*(w, c_i, t_i) \tag{2.19}$$

If this is replaced back in the utility function a conditional indirect utility V_i is obtained.

$$Vi = U\left[W^*(c_i, w, t_i)\right] \tag{2.20}$$

Giving U a Cobb-Douglas form, i.e. $U = K\,G^{1-\beta}L^{\beta}$, using (2.18) we get

$$\frac{\partial U}{\partial W} = (1-\beta)KG^{-\beta}L^{\beta}w - \beta KG^{1-\beta}L^{\beta-1} = 0 \tag{2.21}$$

After some algebraic work the optimal W is found

$$W^* = (1-\beta)(\tau - t_i) + \beta w^{-1}(c_i - E) \tag{2.22}$$

Then, replacing in U, a specific form for V_i is obtained:

$$V_i = K(1-\beta)^{1-\beta}\beta^{\beta}\left[w^{1-\beta}(\tau - t_i) + w^{-\beta}(E - c_i)\right] \tag{2.23}$$

Again, mode choice is decided by comparison among the V_i. This approach yields choices commanded by the maximum value of

$$\overline{U}_i = -K' w^{1-\beta} t_i - K' w^{-\beta} c_i \qquad (2.24)$$

where $$K' = K(1 - \beta)^{1-\beta} \beta^{\beta}$$

Note that $\overline{U}_i$ in equation (2.24) corresponds to what we have called a truncated conditional indirect utility function after the cancellation of additive terms only, involving E and τ. Moreover, when $\beta \rightarrow 0$, then $K'=K$ and choice is determined by $-c_i - wt_i$; and when $\beta \rightarrow 1$, then $K'=K$ and choice follows the maximum of $-\dfrac{c_i}{w} - t_i$. This provides a justification for the specification of cost divided by income in modal utility –sometimes used in practice- where income is in fact a proxy for the wage rate.

Following Definition 2.3, and remembering travel time is a quality with a minus sign (increasing quality means reducing or saving travel time), we can obtain the subjective value of travel time savings from equation (2.23) as

$$SVTTS = \frac{\partial V/\partial t_j}{\partial V/\partial c_j} = w \qquad (2.25)$$

It is important to note that result (2.25) has general validity for model (2.14)-(2.16). From (2.20) and using (2.18) one can get

$$\frac{\partial V_i}{\partial t_i} = -\frac{\partial U}{\partial L} \qquad (2.26)$$

$$\frac{\partial V_i}{\partial c_i} = -\frac{\partial U}{\partial G} \qquad (2.27)$$

and therefore

$$SVTTS = \frac{\partial U / \partial L}{\partial U / \partial G} = w \qquad (2.28)$$

Then, the goods/leisure framework always yields a value of time equal to the (marginal) wage rate given its endogenous income version.

The preceding model includes a rather strong assumption, i.e. that the individual can choose working time freely at a predefined wage rate. Nothing essential changes if a fixed working schedule and a fixed income are introduced in this framework, such that a model with exogenous income I is obtained:

$$\text{Max } U(G,L) \tag{2.29}$$

subject to

$$G + c_i = I \tag{2.30}$$
$$L + W + t_i = \tau \tag{2.31}$$
$$i \in M$$

Under this setting, the trade-off between goods and leisure no longer depends on assigning more or less time to work, but on choosing faster and more expensive modes, or slower and cheaper ones, which is exactly the case depicted in Figure 2.1. In this model, the conditional indirect utility function is directly obtained replacing G and L from the constraints into U, so if we describe utility with a Cobb-Douglas of the form $U = K\, G^{1-\beta}\, L^{\beta}$, then the conditional indirect utility is

$$V_i = K(I - c_i)^{1-\beta}(\tau - W - t_i)^{\beta} \tag{2.32}$$

Now, if the Cobb-Douglas specification is approximated to a second order through a Taylor expansion around $(I, T\text{-}W)$, replacement of G and L plus a convenient rearrangement of terms and simplifying by $K[I/(\tau - w)]^{1-\beta}$, yields a truncated conditional indirect utility function given by (Jara-Díaz, 1998)

$$\overline{U}_i = -(1-\beta)\left[1 + \tfrac{\beta}{2}(S_I - S_T)\right]\frac{ci}{g} - \beta\left[1 + \tfrac{1-\beta}{2}(S_I - S_T)\right]t_i \tag{2.33}$$

where:

$g = \dfrac{I}{\tau - W}$ is an expenditure rate

$S_I = \dfrac{c_i}{I}$ is the share of income spent in transport

$S_T = \dfrac{t_i}{\tau - W}$ is the share of free time spent in transport

(note that $S_I \neq S_T$ always).

The expression for the modal utility represented by equation (2.33) involves a number of novelties. First of all, if either S_I or S_T were significantly different from zero, then second order terms in travel cost, travel time or both, should be included in the specification. This is consistent with a previous observation regarding the role of income in mode choice captured by second order terms in cost (equation (2.12)), because (as should be recalled from the standard theory of consumer behavior) a large share of income in the consumption of a particular good is indicative of the presence of income effect. Secondly, if both S_I and S_T were negligible, a linear specification would be appropriate, keeping some resemblance with the previous version of $\overline{U}_i$ in equation (2.24) which involves the modal cost over the wage rate; in this fixed income case, though, cost is divided by an expenditure rate which represents the amount of money to be spent in a τ-W period (Jara-Díaz and Farah, 1987).

We have named these specifications the **wage rate** and **expenditure rate models** respectively. Note that a fixed working schedule across the population in a sample of fixed income travelers would provide a clear case for the cost over income specification.

The generalized expenditure rate model represented by equation (2.33) helps clarifying an important point regarding the stratification of travelers for model estimation. Imagine that a traditional mode choice model with linear utility is specified with two variables: cost over income, and time; assume as well that individuals in the sample have similar preferences (i.e. same K and β) but trips involve a variety of travel distances (or travel time). This means that individuals in the sample would have different values for S_T and, therefore, different coefficients for cost and time according to equation (2.33). Therefore, different linear models should be estimated for individuals traveling short and long distances. In other words, the sample should be stratified according to distance.

The form that acquires *SVTTS* in the expenditure rate model, i.e. if income is regarded as exogenous, is quite interesting. For the Cobb-Douglas form of direct utility, *SVTTS*, calculated as (2.4) (with a minus sign) and using (2.32) is given by

$$SVTTS = \frac{\beta}{1-\beta} \frac{I - c_i}{\tau - W - t_i} \qquad (2.34)$$

which is nearly proportional to the expenditure rate when c_i and t_i are negligible compared to income and leisure time respectively. In fact, to a first order approximation, *SVTTS* is equal to $g\beta/(1-\beta)$ from the first part of equation (2.33). Note that, for a given income level, a person that works less has a lower value of time. This explains empirical results like those obtained by Bates and Roberts (1986) regarding the low *SVTTS* found for retired individuals. Also, note that *SVTTS* increases with t_i, which means that the (marginal) subjective valuation of travel time increases with trip length. This is an important point as some claim that one additional minute in a short trip should be perceived as more valuable than one additional minute in a long one; this fallacy ignores the fact that what is valuable to an individual is leisure time, which is the complement of t_i. Thus, what matters is the importance of one minute relative to leisure, which diminishes as leisure increases or *increases with travel time*. It is important to note that this is the result usually obtained in empirical studies.

The goods/leisure approach can be used to explore the presumptive relation between income and "pure" or unrestricted preferences, represented by the parameter β in direct utility. If second order effects are assumed negligible and the first order terms are conveniently manipulated when moving from equation (2.32) to equation (2.33), one obtains (Jara-Díaz, 1991)

$$\overline{U}_i = -A\,g^{-\beta}\,c_i - B\,g^{1-\beta}\,t_i \qquad (2.35)$$

which similarity with equation (2.24) is evident. Mode choice models can be estimated to obtain A, B and β for populations with different incomes, in order to examine possible monotonicity between the income level and the estimated β values, i.e. to verify if income and taste are correlated, as some researchers believe. Do low income individuals dislike taxis or luxury cars?

Finally, the appeal of the goods/leisure approach goes beyond its simplicity. It can be adapted to cases like interurban travel or vacation trips to a resort area. Imagine an individual that is self-employed and whose vacations are planned as a long run decision, including destination, duration, and travel mode. In this case the existence of earnings per unit time, and the endogenous decision regarding time spent out of work play a key role in the specification of utility; the resulting model will be similar to a wage rate model. On the other hand, if the individual has a pre-specified vacation period, the expenditure rate approach (properly adapted) could be used, making the vacation budget play the role of fixed income.

2.2.4. Extensions

In applied work, any version of the alternative-specific utility functions introduced here, includes c_i divided by some form of income (e.g. wage rate, income itself or expenditure rate), all components of travel time, other (modal) characteristics, socio-economic indexes, etc. Each variable has a parameter such that MUI and SV_j are easily calculated using equations (2.3) and (2.4) respectively. As discussed, $SVTTS$ under the original version of the goods/leisure trade-off framework is equal to the wage rate, but this is rarely the result in empirical work, in which the ratio of the travel time coefficient over the cost/wage coefficient is usually less than one (a result theoretically supported by Gronau, 1986). This is related with the formulation of the trade-off model, in which the absolute perception of time is captured by the multiplier of the corresponding constraint, which is the same for all activities included in L, for work and for travel. Thus, the price of time is equal for all activities and equal to the wage rate.

The case would be different if restrictions regarding time were identified beyond equation (2.16). One possibility is that of minimum time requirements, like those identified by Truong and Hensher (1985). On the other hand, a ratio significantly greater than one has also been obtained (Jara-Díaz and Ortúzar, 1989). In the latter case, an expenditure rate approach would accept such values as a possibility, as shown in equation (2.34), where $\beta/(1-\beta)$ can take any positive value as β moves within the interval $0 \leq \beta \leq 1$. Note β represents the importance of time in direct utility, which means that individuals with a large absolute perception of time could reveal a high $SVTTS$ if the fixed income, fixed working schedule, is the relevant description of the working condition.

So far, it seemed as if the main issue for the correct specification of (modal) utility was the role of income, its endogeneity or exogeneity, depending on whether paid working hours are decided or not by the individual (see also Viton, 1985). But this narrow approach can be challenged by other approaches where available time and how it is spent plays a key role, as described in the next section.

2.3. Time allocation: a framework for the analysis of time value

2.3.1. Theories

From a microeconomic viewpoint, modeling urban travel demand means introducing time and space in consumer theory. For a given location pattern, an individual has to choose what goods to buy and what activities to perform, potentially including leisure, work and transport. The role of time began to be discussed with special emphasis from 1965 to 1972 in the economic literature. The traditional framework to model consumer behavior sees individuals as trying to achieve the highest level of satisfaction given the constraints faced. As the level of satisfaction was assumed to be dependent on the amount of goods consumed only, the natural constraint was that of a limited purchasing power. The need to understand the labor market made it mandatory to introduce time as an important element in that framework, as the consumer was assumed to face a choice between work and non-work time. When time is considered in consumer theory, there are three important aspects to take into account: first, how time enters the utility function; second, the need to include a time constraint; and third, the need to identify the relations between time allocation and goods consumption. We will see here that each of these aspects plays an important role in the generation of money measures of time assignments.

In what follows, the most important time allocation theories are shown and discussed. The analytical models are synthesized in Table 2.1.

Becker (1965)
In Becker's model, income is essentially an endogenously determined variable, as the individual decides how many hours W to work at a pre-specified wage rate w. If the utility function depends on consumption, and consumption means expenses, it is a natural step to consider that additional time can be assigned to work in order to increase income, but also that this process has a limit because consumption requires time. Becker took this step with a twist: he postulated the idea of "final goods" Z_i as those which directly induced satisfaction, and he focused on market goods and preparation time as necessary inputs for Z_i. His main idea was that work time was in fact total time in a period minus preparation-consumption time. Thus, consuming had a time cost, i.e. the cost of not earning money. This was the origin of a value of time equal to the individual wage rate, irrespective of the specific assignment of time to different types of activity. Note that, from this viewpoint, Train and McFadden's goods/leisure trade-off model is nothing but the discrete counterpart of Becker's.

In modeling terms, in Becker's theory time entered utility as a necessary input to prepare final goods, a time constraint was introduced and then replaced in the income constraint, and the relation between market goods and time was not mentioned at all, although a unit of final good Z_i was said to require goods and time in fixed proportions. Perhaps his emphasis on the conversion of time into money through the wage rate, kept somewhat hidden the implicit fixed conversion coefficients that turned goods into time and vice versa.

Johnson (1966)
Soon after Becker's paper appeared, Johnson established that the reason behind a value of time equal to the wage rate was the absence of work time in the utility function He showed that correcting this omission led to a value of time equal to the wage rate plus the subjective value of work (ratio between the marginal utility of work and the marginal utility of income). Johnson showed that this was equal to the value of leisure, and claimed that, in turn, it was equal to the value of travel time. This, in fact, made sense, as a reduction in travel time could be assigned to either leisure, work or both, but both values should be adjusted until equality through the variation of working hours. But, as shown below, Johnson was missing something as well.

Oort (1969)
Oort mentioned that travel time should be included in utility as well, and a third term appeared in the *SVTTS* notion, namely, the value of the direct perception of travel time in utility. This was also intuitively attractive, as an exogenous reduction in travel time would not only increase leisure or work, but also diminish travel time itself, which might make it even more attractive if travel was not pleasurable directly.

DeSerpa (1971)
In spite of his notation, which actually obscured his results, DeSerpa made a relevant contribution to the value of time discussion by introducing explicitly a set of technical constraints relating time and goods. He postulated a utility function dependent on all goods and all time periods T_i (which he soon called "activities"), including work and travel. The technical constraints established that consumption of a given good required a minimum assignment of time. The model can be written as

$$\text{Max} \quad U = U(X_1, ..., X_n, T_1, ..., T_n) \tag{2.36}$$

subject to:

$$\sum_{i=1}^{n} P_i X_i = I_f \tag{2.37}$$

$$\sum_{i=1}^{n} T_i = \tau \tag{2.38}$$

$$T_i \geq a_i X_i \qquad i = 1, ..., n \tag{2.39}$$

The interpretation of the Lagrange multipliers in non-linear programming establishes that they correspond to the variation of the objective function evaluated at the optimum due to a marginal relaxation of the corresponding restriction. If we denote by λ, μ and K_j the Lagrange multipliers of constraints (2.37) to (2.39), then λ is the marginal utility of income (*MUI*), μ is the *marginal utility of time as a resource* and K_j is the variation of diminishing time required to consume the corresponding good. First order conditions are

$$-\frac{\partial U}{\partial T_j} + \mu - K_j = 0 \qquad (2.40)$$

$$K_i(a_i X_i - T_i) = 0 \qquad (2.41)$$

From (2.40) we obtain

$$\frac{K_j}{\lambda} = \frac{\mu}{\lambda} - \frac{\partial U/\partial T_j}{\lambda} \qquad (2.42)$$

Within this framework, DeSerpa defined three different concepts of time value. The first is **the value of time as a resource**, which is the value of extending the time period, equivalent to the ratio between the marginal utility of total time and the marginal utility of income, μ/λ. The second is the value of assigning time to a specific activity (**value of time as a commodity**), given by the rate of substitution between that activity and money in U, $(\partial U/\partial T_j)/\lambda$. The third concept is the **value of saving time in activity i**, defined as the ratio K_i/λ, where K_i is the multiplier of the corresponding new constraint. Equation (2.42) shows that this ratio is equal to the algebraic difference between the value of time assigned to an alternative use (the resource value) and the value of time as a commodity.

Equation (2.41) is the base of one of his most interesting comments; he defined "leisure" as the sum of all activities which are assigned *more time than strictly necessary* according to the new set of constraints ($T_i > a_i X_i$). For these activities, the corresponding multiplier and the value of saving time (K_i/λ) is zero, necessarily. Therefore, the value of time assigned to each of these activities is equal to μ/λ, the resource value of time or, what is now evident, to the value of leisure time. The intuition behind this is appealing: if the value of assigning time to two activities that are assigned more time than the minimum required was different, the individual would reassign time from the less valuable to the more valuable one until equality holds.

DeSerpa defines the existence of "pure time goods", i.e. those goods that can be described as the time assigned to its "consumption", as is the case of variable work time (T_w), which can be introduced in (2.37) in the form of a good, with price $P_j = -w$, where w is the wage rate. This yields

$$\sum_{i=1}^{n} P_i X_i = I_f + w T_w \qquad (2.43)$$

As T_w appears in two constraints, (2.38) and (2.43), the first order condition related to T_w is

$$-\frac{\partial U}{\partial T_w} + \mu - \lambda w = 0 \qquad (2.44)$$

or

$$\frac{\mu}{\lambda} = w + \frac{\partial U \big/ \partial T_w}{\lambda} \tag{2.45}$$

Equation (2.45) shows the individual assigns time until the value of leisure equals the wage rate plus the value of time assigned to work (value of marginal utility of work). In other words, the value of leisure activities should be equal to the total value of work; otherwise, a reassignment would take place. Introducing (2.45) in (2.42) we get

$$\frac{K_j}{\lambda} = w + \frac{\partial U \big/ \partial T_w}{\lambda} - \frac{\partial U \big/ \partial T_j}{\lambda} \tag{2.46}$$

Equation (2.46) -originally obtained by Oort (1969) in a footnote- says the value of a reduction in the minimum necessary time assigned to a constrained activity (e.g. travel), is equal to the total value of work (equal to the value of leisure) minus the money value of (travel) time in U (value of travel time as a commodity). The main corollary is evident: the value of a reduction in the time assigned to a constrained activity would be equal to the wage rate only if both work and travel do not affect utility directly[8]. Thus, Johnson and Becker results on the value of time are particular cases of results (2.45) and (2.46).

Evans (1972)
Evans was the first to formulate a model for consumer behavior in which utility depended only on time assigned to activities. Consequently, in essence, Evans introduced $U(T)$ as an apparently simple departure from the classical goods consumption model; however, activities are costly because they require goods to be actually performed, and therefore market goods are inputs needed to develop activities and, in turn, goods are the source of the activity cost. If q_{ij} is the input of goods i at a certain rate per unit time which are required for an activity j, then $\sum_j q_{ij} T_j$ is the amount of good i that has to be bought in order to be able to do the activities contained in T, and $P_i \sum_j q_{ij} T_j$ is the expenditure on good i. Thus, the budget constraint is in fact related to QT where Q is the matrix containing the q_{ij} elements. This can be represented as $\sum_j w_j T_j$, where w_j is $\sum_i P_i q_{ij}$. As activities will be interdependent in general, this is taken into account by Evans introducing a matrix J that represents links between activity times through the technical constraints $J'T \le 0$.

The relation $X=QT$ is the first explicit introduction of a transformation function that turns activities into goods (but not vice versa), which was implicitly expressed both in Becker's model (the b_{kj} coefficients in Table 2.1) and in DeSerpa's (the a_i coefficients). For Evans,

---

[8] Of course, there is always the chance that the marginal utilities of work and travel cancel out.

the amount of time to be assigned to each activity is the basic variable, the source of direct utility, and the original source of both expenses and income.

Regarding value of time, Evans made some particularly sharp remarks (he did not seem to be aware of DeSerpa's), beginning with the rejection of the implicit assumption of a zero marginal utility of work in Becker's model. Second, he criticized Johnson (1966) because of the confusion between value of time and value of leisure, extending the critique to Oort (1969), who had compared a reduction in travel time with a day extension. Thirdly, and due to the explicit introduction of a family of constraints dealing with the interrelation among activities, Evans ended up finding the possibility of a zero value for the marginal utility of income for individuals that earn money faster than their capability to spend it; thus, their time constraint is binding and the income constraint is not, which means an infinite value of time as a resource and an infinite value of saving time (but, of course, a finite value for the time allocated to an activity, as it is the money value of its marginal utility).

Small (1982)

Small includes departure time as a variable, which influences utility, travel time and travel cost. The introduction of an institutional constraint that links departure time, working hours and the wage rate, generates a resource value of time that depends on the work schedule.

Gronau (1986)

It is worth mentioning the review on home economics made by Gronau, who in fact extended Becker by including work time in utility. His value of time as a resource ends up being the marginal wage rate plus the value of work, minus the value of work inputs. Gronau's approach does not extend to the value of saving time in an activity, but the introduction of input goods value is indeed a contribution. It should be stressed that Gronau focuses on work at home.

Jara-Díaz (2003)

The technical relations between goods consumed and time devoted to activities was examined in detail in this article, showing that DeSerpa's minimum time requirements for a given consumption bundle was just half of the picture. In fact, Q in Evans' model generates a vector of goods necessary to undertake a given vector of activity times, which can be seen rigorously as minimum consumption requirements. Jara-Díaz made a case for the need to establish not one but two families of relations between goods consumption and time use. This conceptual structure can be established through two general functions: $A(X,T) \geq 0$, the *Activity Possibility Function*, and $G(X,T) \geq 0$, the *Consumption Possibility Function*, where equality defined the Activity Possibility Frontier for a given X in the former, and the Consumption Possibility Frontier for a given T in the latter. This was proposed as a new taxonomy for the technical constraints between goods and time. Their simplest representation could be

$$T_i \geq f_i(X) \tag{2.47}$$

$$X_i \geq g_i(T) \tag{2.48}$$

Transport Economic Theory

The first inequality states that goods consumption imposes minimum levels on activity duration, and the second states that activities impose minimum levels on goods consumption. Jara-Díaz showed that the introduction of these complete set of relations in a time assignment – goods consumption consumer behavior model would generate an additional term in the willingness to pay to reduce a constrained activity (e.g. the *SVTTS*), representing the marginal variation of the (mandatory) consumption structure.

There are other microeconomic models dealing with time allocation and the value of time, like De Donnea (1971), Pollack and Wachter (1975), Michael and Becker (1973), or Dalvi (1978). In Table 2.1 we summarize what we consider the main contributions to the analysis of the value of time.

Table 2.1: Value of time from the main time allocation approaches

Author	Model	2.3.1.1 Value of time
Becker (1965)	$\text{Max} \quad U = U(Z_1,...,Z_n)$ $\sum_{i=1}^{g} P_i X_i = wW + I_f \quad \rightarrow \lambda$ $\sum_{i=1}^{n} T_i = \tau - W \quad \rightarrow \mu$ $T_i = \sum_j a_{ij} Z_j$ $X_k = \sum_j b_{kj} Z_j$	$\dfrac{\mu}{\lambda} = w$
Johnson (1966)	$\text{Max} \quad U = U(L,W,G)$ $G = wW \quad \rightarrow \lambda$ $\tau = L + W \quad \rightarrow \mu$	$\dfrac{\mu}{\lambda} = w + \dfrac{\partial U/\partial W}{\lambda} = \dfrac{\partial U/\partial L}{\lambda}$
Oort (1969)	$\text{Max} \quad U = U(L,W,t,G)$ $\tau = L + W + t \quad \rightarrow \mu$ $G + c = wW \quad \rightarrow \lambda$	$-\dfrac{dU/dt}{\lambda} = w + \dfrac{\partial U/\partial W}{\lambda} - \dfrac{\partial U/\partial t}{\lambda}$ $\dfrac{\mu}{\lambda} = \dfrac{\partial U/\partial L}{\lambda}$
De Serpa (1971)	$\text{Max} \quad U = U(X_1,...,X_n,T_1,...,T_n)$ $\sum_{i=1}^{g} P_i X_i = I_f \quad \rightarrow \lambda$ $\sum_{i=1}^{n} T_i = \tau \quad \rightarrow \mu$ $T_i \geq a_i X_i \quad \rightarrow K_i \quad i = 1,...,n$	$\dfrac{\mu}{\lambda} = \dfrac{\partial U/\partial L}{\lambda}$ $\dfrac{K_i}{\lambda} = \dfrac{\mu}{\lambda} - \dfrac{\partial U/\partial T_i}{\lambda}$
Evans (1972)	$\text{Max} \quad U = U(T_1,...,T_n)$ $\sum_{i=1}^{n} w_i T_i \geq 0 \quad \rightarrow \lambda$ $\tau - \sum_{i=1}^{n} T_i = 0 \quad \rightarrow \mu$	$\dfrac{K_i}{\lambda} = \dfrac{\mu}{\lambda} - \dfrac{\partial U/\partial T_i}{\lambda} - w_i$ $\dfrac{\mu}{\lambda} = \dfrac{\partial U/\partial L}{\lambda} + w_L$

	$T_i - \sum\limits_{\forall\ j\neq i} b_{ij} T_j \geq 0 \quad \rightarrow K_i \quad i=1,...,n$	
Small (1982)	$\text{Max} \quad U = U(G,L,W,s)$ $G + c(s) = I_f + wW \quad \rightarrow \lambda$ $L + t(s) = \tau - W \quad \rightarrow \mu$ $F(s,W;w) = 0 \quad \rightarrow v$	$\dfrac{\mu}{\lambda} = w + \dfrac{\partial U/\partial W}{\lambda} - v\dfrac{\partial F/\partial W}{\lambda}$
Gronau (1986)	$\text{Max} \quad U = U(Z_1,...,Z_n,Z_W)$ $\sum\limits_{i=1}^{g} P_i X_i + P_W X_W = I(Z_W) + I_f \quad \rightarrow$ $\sum\limits_{i=1}^{n} T_i + W = \tau \rightarrow \mu$ $Z_i = f_i(X_i,T_i) \quad i=1...n$ $Z_W = f_W(X_W,W)$	$\dfrac{\mu}{\lambda} = w + \dfrac{\partial U/\partial W}{\lambda} - P_W\dfrac{\partial X_W}{\partial W}$ with $Z_W = W$ and $I(Z_W) = wW$
Jara-Díaz (2003)	$\text{Max} \quad U = U(X_1,...,X_n,T_1,...,T_n)$ $\sum\limits_{i=1}^{g} P_i X_i = wW \quad \rightarrow \lambda$ $\sum\limits_{i=1}^{n} T_i = \tau \quad \rightarrow \mu$ $T_i \geq f_i(X) \quad \rightarrow K_i \quad i=1,...,n$ $X_i \geq g_i(T) \quad \rightarrow \psi_i \quad i=1,...,g$	$\dfrac{K_j}{\lambda} = \dfrac{\mu}{\lambda} - \dfrac{\partial U/\partial T_j}{\lambda} - \dfrac{1}{\lambda}\sum\limits_i \psi_i \dfrac{\partial g_i}{\partial T_j}$

Glossary

T_i : Time assigned to activity i	w : Wage rate (work)
W : Time assigned to work	G : Aggregate consumption in money units
L : Time assigned to leisure	I_f : Individual's fixed income
t_i : Time assigned to travel (mode i)	τ : Total time available
t : Exogenous travel time	U : Utility function
c_i : Travel cost (mode i)	F : Function that accounts for the limitations imposed by the institutional setting within witch employment opportunities are encountered.
c : Travel cost	S : Schedule time (a specific time of the day)
Z_i : Final good i	μ : Multiplier of time restriction
f_i : Production function of commodity i	λ : Multiplier of income restriction
P_i : Price of good i	v : Multiplier of schedule restriction
X_i : Consumption of good i	K_i : Multiplier of minimum time requirement of activity i
P_W : Price of goods for work activity (nursery, travel, etc)	b_{ij} : Minimum time requirement of activity i per unit of activity j
X_W : Consumption of goods associated with work activity	ψ_i : Multiplier of minimum consumption requirement of good i.
w_i : Money reward of activity i	$f_{fi}(X)$: Minimum time for activity i as a function of goods.
w_L : Money reward of Leisure	$g(T)$: Minimum consumption of good i as a function of activities.

2.3.2. Discussion

As seen, time evolved in consumption theory from a secondary role to a central one in a short period. However, today the basic approach to model consumer behavior still rests on the idea of goods consumption as the primary source of direct utility. If one looks at Table 2.1 trying to make a synthesis, there are some key issues to highlight. The first one is the relation between goods and time, the type of relation that was explicitly introduced by DeSerpa. Such a relation is fairly general in both Becker's and Evans' models through a_{ij} and b_{kj} in the first one and Q in the second. All of these relations can be synthesized in a general framework which encompasses the ones found in the literature. The point is that both minimum time and minimum consumption technical requirements need to be established.

The second issue to discuss is the presence (or absence) of working time W (T_w in DeSerpa's notation) in the direct utility function. Both DeSerpa and Evans include working hours as a direct source of utility, unlike Becker, who explicitly leaves W out. This is an important matter, as including working hours in utility would make Becker's synthesis of income and time constraints into one a mistake, because W could not "disappear" from the constraints since the utility level would be affected. If no technical restrictions linking consumption and time are taken into account, the value of time would be equal for all activities because time is adjusted accordingly. And this leads to the third issue, which is more ample than specific minimum time requirements: the interrelation among activities. This is explicit in Evans' model only, although DeSerpa introduces an idea which, as explained here, is somewhat related to the notion of a transformation function representing the relation between goods and time. This interrelation is the source of the relative importance of different activities from an analytical viewpoint; as this differential perception of activities is in fact observed, omitting such a constraint would yield to limited models. Note, however, that accounting for technical constraints (2.47) and (2.48) could also induce different valuation among leisure activities as shown in Jara-Díaz (2003).

The approach each researcher took to view time and its relation to utility is relevant. For Becker, T is time to prepare the final commodities (which is the reason why W is left out of utility); for DeSerpa, T is consumption time; for Train and McFadden, the aggregate source of utility is leisure; Truong and Hensher include travel time in direct utility in the so-called DeSerpa model. As particularly emphasized by Evans, Bates (1987) and Gronau, including or not an activity time in direct utility plays a key role in the interpretation of a model. We concur. In analytical terms, the behavior represented by the corresponding first order conditions for optimality, might include or not a marginal utility of time assigned to the particular activity in question. If we are to judge the conceptual validity of these models, the basic question is whether the individual level of satisfaction can change only because of transfers among leisure, work and travel, through the time constraint with an impact on purchasing power, or also due to pleasure or displeasure generated directly by spending time in something.

In this regard, it is a striking fact that Evans' model can be stated in terms of activity times *only*. This is certainly noteworthy considering the fundamental approach of consumer behavior theory, where emphasis is on goods. Can this model be converted into a goods consumption model? It appears to be possible, but only in special cases, when Q is invertible, according to the conversion of times T into goods X, $T=Q^{-1}X$, but in the general case Q is not necessarily square, leave alone invertible. Even if the conversion is allowed, the two other constraints still remain: the total time constraint, and a set of linked-activity type constraints. The resulting commodity consumption model is, therefore, a different one. Yet, being transformable or not should not deviate our attention from Evans' model key characteristic, that is, being time-oriented; Evans argues in favor of *time devoted to activities* as the basic quantifiable source of utility.

Keeping the previous point on hold, we should make another important remark, now regarding goods/leisure and Becker's models, by realizing that both provide the same value of time: the wage rate. It should really be no surprise, as in both cases three conditions concur: income is endogenously determined by freely choosing working hours, these do not affect direct utility, and no constraints besides income and time budgets are included. So even though they look different and their utilities have different foundations, the two models are in fact conceptually the same.

The preceding comment makes Gronau's extension of Becker's work more relevant than originally assumed. By association, a generalized version of the goods/leisure model can be constructed, simply replacing W in equation (2.16) by W_F+W_V representing fixed and variable (endogenously decided) working hours respectively, and putting $W=W_V$ and $E=I$ (fixed income) in equation (2.15). Such a model still would be lacking work in direct utility, but both the wage rate and expenditure rate specifications could be obtained as particular cases, using W_V as pivot; if W_V results with a positive value, the wage rate approach holds, and a zero value (corner solution) implies an expenditure rate model. Note that the endogeneity of marginal working hours is something that can be observed.

These associations between Gronau's, Becker's and goods/leisure models, plus the remark on the activities-oriented nature of Evans' model, should not be overlooked, as a common ground seems to dominate the picture: DeSerpa establishes that activities, including work, enter utility directly; Evans does the same; and Gronau generalizes Becker's model by plugging a "work activity" in utility, but more broadly, defining utility in terms of a set of Z_i's, which eventually he defined as activities. It seems all roads lead to Rome.

2.4. A unified travel-activities model

2.4.1. The approach

An appropriate view of individual behavior from a microeconomic perspective should rest on activities as the primary source of utility. This implies looking at goods as means necessary to actually realize a set of activities. Doing that requires the introduction of a conversion or transformation function turning activity times into goods and vice versa. A relation between activity times themselves seems to be necessary as well. This means that introducing time in a microeconomic framework goes beyond the addition of a time constraint. Moreover, time should not be seen as the number of minutes necessary to either

Transport Economic Theory

prepare a final good or consume a market commodity; it is the direct source of utility by means of being assigned to activities.

Note that this apparently innocent change of perspective moves things in a different direction. First, the primary result of a consumer model would include "activity demand functions" (in addition to market demands for goods) and second, if a $U(X,T)$ type of utility was taken as a correct formulation, an explanation should be given for the presence of X (as opposed to that of T). One possible explanation would be the qualitative content of a certain type of activity, i.e. the marginal utility of activity i could depend on the type and amount of goods used, making $\partial^2 U / \partial T_i \partial X_j$ different from zero. Note this would depend solely on the degree of detail used to describe an activity (e.g. dinning poorly versus dinning abundantly).

It seems that there has been an emphasis on keeping as arguments in utility only those elements which are believed to increase satisfaction (e.g. leisure, goods). Somehow the idea of non-leisure activities as direct arguments has been postponed, despite the previous examples and discussions. To test whether a variable should enter U, the problem can be restated as follows: if *everything* else is kept constant, would a change in that variable induce a change in satisfaction? Note that this is unrelated to feasibility, particularly regarding time. Remember that the marginal utility of available time (μ) measures the variation in utility *if* total time available increased. Although this is not feasible, the multiplier has a value. Then we can ask whether a change in utility would occur if some activity time increased, *everything else kept constant.*

We find no reason for an arbitrarily asymmetric treatment of activities. Thus, all particularly identifiable activities should enter U, as separate entities, including work and travel time. On the other hand, the pleasure induced by the consumption of a certain good is always realized through some activity. Even if some goods are bought for the pleasure of acquiring, satisfaction is realized in the act of buying; if it is a piece of art, satisfaction is experienced by the act of admiring or by enhancing an action (either at work or at ease). However, the marginal utility of an activity indeed varies depending on the type and amount of goods consumed, e.g. having a more comfortable bed increases the satisfaction of sleeping as a grossly described activity, or eating tastier food increases the pleasure of eating, at a rate that depends on the amount eaten. **In the end, everything suggests the appropriate specification for the direct utility function is $U(T,X)$.**

2.4.2. The formulation

After looking at the microeconomics of mode choice models and time allocation literature, a unified model can be proposed. In a general model encompassing activities and goods, four types of relations have to be taken into account. First, the source of individual satisfaction (utility) is primarily the time devoted to each activity, including *all* activities (sleep, eat, talk, travel, work, and so on), and the amount and type of goods consumed on each activity. Second, a budget constraint that accounts for all expenses and all types of income. Third, a time constraint accounting for total activity times limited by social and biological cycles (days, weeks, months). Fourth, technical constraints establishing minimum goods consumption and minimum time assignments. A general model should look like

$$\text{Max } U(T,X)$$

Subject to:

Income constraint

Time constraint

Technological constraints

The following practical model accounts for all these dimensions in a complete though analytically workable framework. Let T_i be the time assigned to activity i and X_j the amount of good j consumed during period τ, with minima given by T_i^{Min} and X_j^{Min}, respectively. Define T_w as the time assigned to work, P_j as the price of good j, w as the wage rate, and I_f as the exogenous fixed income. If utility is given a generalized Cobb-Douglas form where Ω is a positive constant and η_j and θ_i are the exponents associated with good j and activity i respectively, then consumer behavior can be seen as if time assignment and goods consumption was commanded by

$$\text{Max } \quad U = \Omega T_w^{\theta_w} \prod_i T_i^{\theta_i} \prod_j X_j^{\eta_j} \tag{2.49}$$

subject to

$$I_f + wT_w - \sum_j P_j X_j \geq 0 \tag{2.50}$$

$$\tau - T_w - \sum_i T_i = 0 \tag{2.51}$$

$$T_i - T_i^{Min.} \geq 0 \ \forall i \tag{2.52}$$

$$X_j - X_j^{Min} \geq 0 \ \forall j \tag{2.53}$$

with Lagrange multipliers λ, μ, κ_i and φ_i respectively. As explained earlier, μ / λ is the value of time as a resource or value of leisure. Although the technical constraints take the simplest possible form, they will prove to be quite important.

At equilibrium, let F be the set of freely chosen activities, R the set of activities assigned the minimum required T_r^{Min}, K the set of freely chosen goods, and J the set of goods of which the minimum required X_j^{Min} is consumed. Define

$$G_f = \left(\sum_{j \in J} P_j X_j^{Min} - I_f \right) \quad \text{and} \quad T_f = \sum_{r \in R} T_r^{Min.} \tag{2.54}$$

The first order conditions for goods are:

$$\frac{\eta_k U}{X_k} - \lambda P_k = 0 \ \forall k \in K \tag{2.55}$$

$$\frac{\eta_j U}{X_j^{Min.}} + \varphi_j - \lambda P_j = 0 \quad \forall j \in J \tag{2.56}$$

For activities other than work,

$$\frac{\theta_i U}{T_i} - \mu = 0 \quad \forall i \in F \tag{2.57}$$

$$\frac{\theta_r U}{T_r^{Min}} + \kappa_r - \mu = 0 \quad \forall r \in R \tag{2.58}$$

and for work,

$$\frac{\theta_w U}{T_w} + \lambda w - \mu = 0 \tag{2.59}$$

Note that unconstrained activities (those that are freely assigned more time than the minimum) must have equal positive marginal utilities (all equal to μ), otherwise they would not be undertaken. Besides, every unpleasant activity will be assigned the exogenous minimum, because the sign of its marginal utility is the same irrespective of duration under this specification. This does not mean that an activity that is assigned the minimum time is necessarily unpleasant, because the optimal time assignment could be less than the exogenous minimum. First order conditions for all activities in F plus constraints (2.51) and (2.52) yield

$$\frac{\mu}{U} = \frac{A}{\left(\tau - T_w - T_f\right)} \tag{2.60}$$

where A is the summation of the exponents over all unrestricted activities. Note that the denominator is simply the uncommitted time. Similarly, if B is the summation of the exponents over all unrestricted goods, first order conditions over all goods in K plus constraints (2.50) and (2.53) yield

$$\frac{\lambda}{U} = \frac{B}{\left(wT_w - G_f\right)} \tag{2.61}$$

Replacing (2.60) and (2.61) in (2.59) an equation is obtained for T_w

$$\frac{\theta_w}{T_w} + w\frac{B}{\left(wT_w - G_f\right)} - \frac{A}{\left(\tau - T_w - T_f\right)} = 0 \tag{2.62}$$

Define

$$\alpha \equiv \frac{\left(A + \theta_w\right)}{2\left(A + B + \theta_w\right)} \qquad\qquad \beta \equiv \frac{\left(B + \theta_w\right)}{2\left(A + B + \theta_w\right)} \tag{2.63}$$

$$\gamma_i \equiv \frac{\theta_i}{\left(A + B + \theta_w\right)} \quad \forall i \in F \qquad \rho_k \equiv \frac{\eta_k}{\left(A + B + \theta_w\right)} \quad \forall k \in K \tag{2.64}$$

Note definitions (2.63) and (2.64) do nothing but normalize utility in equation (2.49), which keeps the results invariant, as it is a monotonic transformatio n of the objective function. Although it is usual to do it such that the sum over all exponents equals unity in a Cobb-Douglas utility function, these definitions have a clearer interpretation.

Equation (2.62) has two roots, but a straightforward analysis of the case where $\theta_w = 0$ shows that only one solution is valid, which is given by equation (2.65).

$$T_w^* = \beta(\tau - T_f) + \alpha \frac{G_f}{w} + \sqrt{\left[\beta(\tau - T_f) + \alpha \frac{G_f}{w}\right]^2 - (2\alpha + 2\beta - 1)(\tau - T_f)\frac{G_f}{w}} \qquad (2.65)$$

Using this result and equations (2.56), (2.59), (2.54) and (2.61) yield

$$T_i^* = \frac{\gamma_i}{(1-2\beta)}\left(\tau - T_w^* - T_f\right) \qquad \forall i \in F \qquad (2.66)$$

$$X_k^* = \frac{\rho_k}{P_k(1-2\alpha)}\left(wT_w^* - G_f\right) \qquad \forall k \in K \qquad (2.67)$$

Equation (2.65) yields working hours assigned by the individual as a function of uncommitted time, uncommitted expenses, and the wage rate: the individual labor supply, which can be compared with equation (2.22) that corresponds to the very simple goods-leisure view. Equations (2.66) and (2.67) correspond to the demand for time assigned to activities and for goods, respectively. Note equation (2.67) can be trivially expressed as expenditure in the k-th good by simply moving price to the left hand side.

2.4.3. Estimation and values of time

Equation (2.65) involves a and β as parameters to be estimated. Equation (2.66) adds one parameter (γ_i) to be estimated for each freely chosen activity i. In the same way, equation (2.67) adds one parameter (ρ_k) for each goods consumption equation included. Because of the restrictions on consumption and time, only up to n-1 time assignment or good consumption models can be estimated (with n the cardinal of the corresponding set of unrestricted activities or goods), otherwise linear dependency would be introduced as the equations add up to total time or income available respectively. In many cases one does not know exactly which activities (or goods) are restricted, which is something that can be explored empirically. Although a and β can be estimated using equation (2.65) only, they would be more efficiently estimated together with γ_i and ρ_k using equations (2.66) and (2.67). Note that, depending on the available information, one can choose to estimate the whole system of equations or a subset, as for example labor supply and activities.

One of the advantages of the model system as derived here is that data can be accommodated to different degrees of aggregation in the variables, because adding

Transport Economic Theory

activities (or goods) does not change the structure of the model. This can be observed directly from the definition of both A and B, which can be associated with the exponents of leisure and a generalized good respectively in a fully aggregated goods-leisure-work-restricted activities model. But the most interesting property of the model is the empirical estimation of the value of leisure and the value of assigning time to work. From equations (2.60) and (2.61) and the definitions of α and β one gets the following expressions of the value of leisure:

$$\frac{\mu}{\lambda} = \frac{A}{B} \frac{\left(w T_w^* - G_f \right)}{\left(\tau - T_w^* - T_f \right)} = \frac{1 - 2\beta}{1 - 2\alpha} \frac{\left(w T_w^* - G_f \right)}{\left(\tau - T_w^* - T_f \right)} \tag{2.68}$$

On the other hand, recalling that the marginal utility of work time is given by $U\theta_w / T_w$ and using equation (2.61) to solve for U, the value of time assigned to work happens to be given by

$$\frac{\partial U / \partial T_w}{\lambda} = \frac{\theta_w}{B} \frac{\left(w T_w^* - G_f \right)}{T_w^*} = \frac{2\alpha + 2\beta - 1}{1 - 2\alpha} \frac{\left(w T_w^* - G_f \right)}{T_w^*} \tag{2.69}$$

The definitions of A, B and θ_w provide intuition for these results, as the value of leisure increases with the relative importance of leisure activities in utility and with what we called **expenditure rate** within the goods/leisure framework, defined after equation (2.33). Similarly, the value of work increases with its relative importance in utility and with the wage rate, as clearly seen in the case where G_f is nil.

2.4.4. Discrete travel choices

Let us see now how a discrete choice model can be obtained from this general model of activity time assignment and goods consumption. Just as is done in the goods-leisure model, the indirect utility function can be obtained by replacing the equations for optimal work (2.65), leisure activities (2.66) and consumption (2.67) in the direct utility function (2.49). As the problem is invariant to monotonic transformations of utility, we can normalize by taking root $(A+B+\theta_w)$. Using definitions (2.63), all this yields

$$V = \tilde{\Omega} w^{1-2\alpha} \left(T_w^* - \frac{G_f}{w} \right)^{1-2\alpha} \left(\tau - T_w^* - T_f \right)^{1-2\beta} T_w^{*2\alpha+2\beta-1} \prod_{r \in R} T_r^{Min \gamma_r} \prod_{j \in J} X_j^{Min \cdot P_j} \tag{2.70}$$

where $\tilde{\Omega}$ collects several constant terms and is better expressed as a function of the original parameters, i.e.

$$\tilde{\Omega} = \left(\frac{\Omega}{A^A B^B} \prod_{k \in K} \left(\frac{\eta_k}{P_k} \right)^{\eta_k} \prod_{i \in I} (\theta_i)^{\theta_i} \right)^{\frac{1}{A+B+\theta_w}} \tag{2.71}$$

This expression for V represents the maximum achievable utility with a wage rate w, fixed expenses G_f and time assigned to constrained activities T_f. Let one of these activities be travel, such that the individual has to chose among several alternatives, each one characterized by travel time t_i and cost c_i. In this case, expression (2.70) can be transformed trivially into a conditional indirect utility function V_i by simple considering t_i and c_i explicitly as part of T_f and G_f respectively, i.e.

$$G_f = G_f' + c_i \qquad T_f = T_f' + t_i \qquad (2.72)$$

$$V_i = \tilde{\Omega} w^{1-2\alpha} \left(T_w^* - \frac{G_f'}{w} - \frac{c_i}{w} \right)^{1-2\alpha} \left(\tau - T_w^* - T_f' - t_i \right)^{1-2\beta} T_w^{*2\alpha + 2\beta - 1} \prod_{r \in R} T_r^{Min\gamma_r} \prod_{j \in J} X_j^{Min.\rho_i} \quad (2.73)$$

This way the resulting function $V_i(t_i, c_i, w, G_f', T_f')$ is, by definition, the maximum utility achievable conditional in the i-th alternative, and can be estimated using known econometric procedures. The independent variables are: total time assigned to all constrained activities *but* travel, expenses in mandatory (restricted) goods *but* travel, the wage rate, and the cost and travel time of each discrete alternative. Note that when estimating simplified versions of V_i, say linear for each of several population segments, the variables w, G_f' and T_f' could be used to stratify properly.

From the discrete model one can calculate the value of saving travel time in the usual way as the ratio between $\partial V_i / \partial t_i$ and $\partial V_i / \partial c_i$ evaluated in the chosen alternative e. By construction this is an estimate of κ_i / λ in the original problem. Then using equation (2.42) the value of time assigned to travel (i.e. the value of its marginal utility) can be obtained as the difference with the value of leisure estimated with equation (2.68), i.e.

$$\frac{\partial U / \partial T_i}{\lambda} = \frac{\mu}{\lambda} - \frac{\kappa_i}{\lambda} = \frac{(1-2\beta)(wT_w^* - G_f)}{(1-2\alpha)(\tau - T_w^* - T_f)} - \frac{\partial V_e / \partial t_e}{\partial V_e / \partial c_e} \qquad (2.74)$$

The system composed of equations (2.65), (2.66), (2.67) and (2.73) constitute a powerful approach to model work, activities, consumption and travel and to estimate all relevant components of the value of time. What is important is to recognize that the conditional indirect utility function that commands travel choice should be consistent with the equations representing labor supply, time assignment and consumption. Note that this approach to obtain a discrete travel choice model can be applied to as many restricted activities as wanted.

2.4.5. Comments

The proposed framework to understand travel behavior rests on DeSerpa's view as a gross construct, and also on the goods/leisure version of the discrete choice approach, but significantly departures from both. Accordingly, it should be no surprise that a wage rate type specification for modal utility is recovered when a mode choice decision is derived under the appropriate assumptions, provided that variable working hours exist. At this point, it seems fairly clear that the role of labor supply is highly relevant: if it is fixed (exogenous income, at least in the short run), what matters is the time available to spend the money, while if it is variable (endogenous income), marginal adjustments make the wage rate a key variable. Some additional properties of the travel model are:

a) travel and activities time allocation are decisions that belong to the same class;

b) the subjective value of each constrained activity can be different;

c) if income is relatively small, choices in time space can be very limited because of the relations between goods and activities, which can make the time constraint irrelevant;

d) if income is relatively large, a number of activities are open for consideration because the necessary goods and services could be acquired. This could make the income constraint irrelevant.

An approach like the one presented here puts the emphasis on time allocation and, therefore, on the perception of time. Decisions on what to do within a time frame become the relevant phenomenon to investigate. Part of this deals with the analysis of labor supply (how much to work), but understanding individual time allocation as a whole requires a very deep look at human activities. Maybe analyzing travel decisions does not require understanding the profound motives behind the search for wealth, fame or power, but the influence of dominant social values is indeed relevant when studying the structure of daily activities. This makes it important the identification of socially induced activities, telecommunication, or the relations between prices and uses of goods (e.g. in addition to the "do I have money?" question, add the "do I have extra time to use it?", or "what will I stop doing in order to use this?"). Thus, acquiring cable TV, having a compact disc player in the car or playing soccer with the neighbors, become something relevant to understand and model. On the other hand, there is a need to understand activity choice when income is small enough to rule out the acquisition of leisure goods (e.g. toys, gadgets) or the admission to leisure activities (e.g. movies, sports). This might have an impact on new types of segmentation, between those that still have money when the day ends, and those that still have day when they run out of money. Needless to say, the aggregate trends on social behavior, the role of technology and social values, or social idiosyncrasy, seem essential to understand travel.

2.5. Synthesis

Consumer theory essentially provides a framework to describe economic behavior. Within this framework, the concept of utility function has been instrumental to model demand for goods and services. Although travel demand has benefited from this framework, it seemed necessary to make a revision of the specific way in which the general framework has been adapted to understand and model transport users' behavior. Travel choices have been examined from the perspective of consumer theory, in an attempt to unveil the specific role of the different elements taking part in users' decisions.

Discrete choices, the goods/leisure approach, and time-related theories of behavior have been exposed and examined as contributors of a general framework for travel decisions. From this analysis on the microeconomic foundations of models related to trip decisions, some issues have been clearly established. First it is the question about the sources of direct utility; starting from goods consumed and going through the concept of basic commodities, consumption time appeared as a *necessary* item to realize utility. After this modest beginning, time devoted to activities emerged as *the* basic source of satisfaction, and it is goods that should be looked at as means to an end. Once this is accepted, every single minute in a period should be considered. This means, among other things, that both working and travel times are variables that should enter utility just as all other activities. Time cannot be converted into money (through more work) without altering utility, which makes the fusion of income and time constraints a mistake.

Clearly, the traditional time and budget constraints are not enough to complete the picture for individual behavior, as market goods and activity times are interrelated (as are activities themselves as well). The addition of a set of technical constraints is necessary to strengthen the fact that activities require goods and goods require time. It is a fact that no explicit reference to a transformation function has been made so far within the context of time allocation models, although recent developments have attempted to formalize this, leading to improved versions of time values (Jara-Díaz, 2003).

Discrete choice theory in the form of mode choice models facilitates the calculation of the subjective value of travel time as the marginal rate of substitution between travel cost and travel time (for different type of individuals and circumstances). This subjective value can incorporate various elements, depending on the complete effect of a travel time reduction on the individual. Synthetically, there are four important effects: the potential increase in purchasing power, the substitution for pleasurable activities, the direct (dis) satisfaction of work, and the direct (dis) satisfaction of the trip itself.

It is somewhat surprising to realize that little discussion has taken place regarding the variables included in direct utility. In fact, goods and services seemed a reasonable choice until the recognition of a time constraint. The introduction of such a constraint implies relations between goods and activities that cannot be overlooked. Moreover, once this has been firmly established, identifying the assignment of time to activities as the basic source of satisfaction seems evident. Interestingly, this gives urban travel a different status. Activities related to personal care (eating, sleeping and other biological needs) consumes in average a little more than eleven hours daily. A normal working schedule would leave something like four hours for discretionary activities on a working day. In such context, time assigned to mandatory urban travel can consume a relevant part of this potentially uncommitted time, so understanding travel demand means understanding activities. In the home production literature, the role of travel has been highlighted already. *"The shadow price of time affects customer's choice of the optimum combination of time and market inputs and the decision whether to participate in market work or not. The imputation of this shadow price is therefore based on the observation of choices where time is traded for goods, and the choice concerning labor force participation. Unfortunately, most often in situations where goods are traded for time, the amount of time saved is unrecorded [...] One of the few exceptions is the field of transportation"* (Gronau, 1986, pp. 292).

Although a framework does not necessarily translate immediately into an operational model, implementation should be kept in mind. For example, an activity-travel model as the one proposed here yields conditional demands for goods, work and activities as intermediate results when modeling mode choice. All variables are potentially known, and a system of equations could be estimated, as done by Jara-Díaz and Guevara (2003). Undoubtedly, there has been a historical emphasis on market demand for goods, a bias that has blurred the activity-oriented approaches. Maybe the present universal trend towards the "I have no time" syndrome will reverse the situation.

3. Valuation of users' benefits in transport systems

3.1. Introduction

Other things being constant, cheaper, faster, safer or more comfortable forms of transport make people feel better off. But improving transport systems requires funding which could have been assigned to other important needs. Benefits of better transport are behind the former phenomenon; costs are behind the latter. This means happiness on one hand, resources on the other. We need to express a change in well-being in monetary terms, so we can compare that value with costs in order to determine if a project is worth the effort, and if so, rank it within a set of alternatives, which is a common and very important part of regional and urban planning processes. It is indeed as challenging as it sounds, but the only other option is to just fund and build the projects and then hope for the best, which does not sound very appealing.

We will begin by presenting the simplest and most common measures to estimate user benefits, the Marshallian consumer's surplus and its approximation, the Rule-of-the-Half (*RH*), including the necessary conditions demand functions must fulfill to use them and providing examples with entropy and Logit models. As will be shown, though, these measures are justified on purely intuitive grounds, a fact that raises a question about their validity. To examine this issue, we will search for a rigorous measure to valuate user benefits, starting from the very foundations of the neo-classical economic theory. Such analysis will show that there is not one, but two correct measures available, the Equivalent Variation (*EV*) and the Compensating Variation (*CV*), which actually do not match the results provided by the Marshall's measure or *RH* unless some conditions are satisfied.

What is interesting is that under certain conditions, the Marshallian Surplus and *RH* provide a reasonable approximation to *EV* and *CV* values, and that is a key finding for practical applications. Furthermore, the relationship between these four measures will prove useful to examine an issue that is normally neglected in developed countries but of high interest in developing ones, namely the role of household or personal income in benefits valuation.

Once we have reviewed how to estimate transport user benefits, it will be necessary to address another question that typically arises in this topic: Are we really considering *all* benefits? Users may benefit from a transport project, but if so, we could rightfully wonder if other activities are also benefiting as a collateral effect.

The chapter ends with the rather important matter of weighting and aggregating user benefits for public decision-making: We may have estimates for user benefits, but we know each person perceives its individual benefit differently because they value their time differently, as was already discussed in the previous chapter. So, establishing a project's benefits necessarily implies combining these different individually perceived benefits in a specific way, which in time implies a particular view about how important the benefit of each particular person is to the whole of society. If tax money is going to finance a project, then it is of great importance to examine what kind of weights we are assigning to each individual or group.

3.2.   Traditional approaches

3.2.1. The Marshallian consumer's surplus

Marshall (1920) defined consumer's surplus as *'the excess of the price which [the consumer] would be willing to pay rather than go without the thing, over that which he actually does pay'*. So the concept was born in terms of one good and its price. The classical textbook drawing represents the Marshallian consumer's surplus (MCS) in the price-good (P_i, X_i) space as the area below the demand curve, above the actual price level. This is said to reflect the total willingness to pay minus actual payment. After a price variation, the change in MCS is graphically represented as the area bounded by the demand curve between the two price levels. Thus, we can define a measure of users' benefits in the following way:

Definition 3.1: Marshallian consumers' surplus variation
If P_i varies from P_i^0 to P_i^1, then the variation of Marshallian consumers' surplus is given by

$$\Delta MCS = - \int_{P_i^0}^{P_i^1} X_i dP_i \tag{3.1}$$

The definition is set in such a way that ΔMCS is positive for a price drop. Note equation (3.1) requires all other prices (and personal income) to remain constant, since demand is known to depend on all those variables.

Hotelling (1938) provided a generalization of this consumer's surplus measure to variations in more than one price, proposing a line integral,

$$\Delta MCS = - \int_{P^0}^{P^1} \sum_i X_i(P, I) dP_i \tag{3.2}$$

Equation (3.2) in principle is an operational measure that can be computed for practical purposes. It is stated in terms of market demands which are observable, and can be estimated and integrated. However, for the line integral (3.2) to have a unique value, market demands have to fulfill the following conditions (Green's theorem):

$$\frac{\partial X_i}{\partial P_j} = \frac{\partial X_j}{\partial P_i} \quad i \neq j \tag{3.3}$$

When this condition is not present, the value of ΔMCS depends on the path of integration from P^0 to P^1, which is an unfortunate result.

Despite this limitation, Marshall's measure has become the favorite choice to assess users' benefits. That said, it is important to mention that it is common for practitioners not to estimate ΔMCS directly, but to calculate an approximation of it instead; the so-called Rule-of-a-Half.

3.2.2. The rule-of-a-half

The rule-of-a-half (RH) is the most widely used form of measuring users' benefits in transport projects and it was supported, at first, on a purely intuitive argument (Neuberger 1971): Let T^0 and T^1 denote the number of trips between a given pair of zones (by a certain mode or alternative) in some initial and final situations, respectively. Let C^0 and C^1 be the corresponding unitary costs of those trips. It will be arbitrarily assumed that $C^1<C^0$ and, therefore, $T^1>T^0$. The intuitive reasoning begins by dividing users in two classes: those who remain traveling between the two zones, before and after the cost reduction, and the 'new' users. Obviously, there will be T^0 'old' users and (T^1 - T^0) new ones.

It follows directly that old users' benefit is $T^0(C^0$ - $C^1)$. Furthermore, a new user cannot perceive a benefit greater than (C^0 - C^1) nor less than zero. Then, if a linearity assumption is made for the individual benefit of *new* users, i.e. benefits are assumed to lie halfway between these two extremes, the total benefit for them will be $(T^1-T^0)\cdot\frac{1}{2}(C^0-C^1)$. So, the (Marshallian) consumers' surplus variation can be written as

$$\Delta MCS \approx T^0\left(C^0-C^1\right)+\left(T^1-T^0\right)\cdot\tfrac{1}{2}\left(C^0-C^1\right) \tag{3.4}$$

which simplifies to the well-known expression of the RH for one pair of origin-destination (O-D) zones and one mode:

$$\Delta MCS \approx \tfrac{1}{2}\left(T^0+T^1\right)\left(C^0-C^1\right) \tag{3.5}$$

A graphical interpretation of this argument is given in Figure 3.1. Consumers' surplus is represented here by the area C^0-A-C-B-C^1 (joining points A and B through the demand curve), while RH quantifies the area C^0-A-C'-B-C^1 (joining A and B by a straight line). Obviously, the less curved the demand, the better the approximation obtained with RH. **In other words, this figure tells us RH is a good measure of Marshallian user's benefit when dealing with marginal changes of costs.**

In order to obtain a more general expression, let T_{ijk} be the number of trips from zone i to zone j by mode k, and let C_{ijk} be the unitary cost of a trip from zone i to zone j by mode k. If n is the total number of zones and M the total number of modes available for users, it should be clear RH may be written as:

$$\Delta MCS \approx \frac{1}{2}\sum_{i=1}^{n}\sum_{j=1}^{n}\sum_{k=1}^{M}\left(T_{ijk}^0+T_{ijk}^1\right)\left(C_{ijk}^0-C_{ijk}^1\right) \tag{3.6}$$

Transport Economic Theory

where superscripts 0 and 1 refer to the initial and final situations[9].

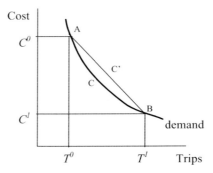

Figure 3.1. *Graphical interpretation of the rule-of-a-half for one mode and one O-D pair.*

Changes may occur in several interzonal costs, and in one or more modes, while demand for trips in a given mode between a given pair of zones depends, in general, on the perceived costs of the other modes that serve not only that O-D pair, but other pairs as well. For each mode and O-D pair, users can again be divided into two classes: those who remain traveling between the same origin and destination in the same mode, and those who modify their behavior responding to the change. For trips between origin i and destination j, users of the first type will perceive benefits given by $T_{ijk}^0 \left(C_{ijk}^1 - C_{ijk}^0 \right)$ since T_{ijk}^0 is the number of users that do not change their choice. The second part of the benefits is associated to those who do change. In order to simplify the explanation, consider the particular case of those users who travel from i to j by mode a before the change, and from i to h by mode b afterwards. These users will appear twice in the expression (3.7), as part of both T_{ija}^0 and T_{ihb}^1. Assuming for simplicity $\left(C_{ihb}^0 - C_{ihb}^1 \right) > \left(C_{ija}^0 - C_{ija}^1 \right)$, benefits for this type of users cannot be larger than $\left(C_{ihb}^0 - C_{ihb}^1 \right)$, nor less than $\left(C_{ija}^0 - C_{ija}^1 \right)$. If benefits are assumed to lie halfway between these two extremes, it is easy to obtain expression (3.6) by simple addition of the two types of benefits for all O-D pairs and modes. This result can also be expressed in terms of flows and costs on links of the corresponding network, i.e.

$$\Delta MCS = \frac{1}{2} \left[\sum_{k \in K} \sum_{m=1}^{M} \left(N_{km}^0 C_{km}^0 + N_{km}^1 C_{km}^0 \right) - \sum_{l \in L} \sum_{m=1}^{M} \left(N_{lm}^0 C_{lm}^1 + N_{lm}^1 C_{lm}^1 \right) \right] \tag{3.7}$$

---

[9] Strictly, the number of modes available for users of a certain socio economic group varies from one pair of origin destination zones to another. The expression must be:

$$\Delta MCS = \frac{1}{2} \sum_{i=1}^{n} \sum_{j=1}^{n} \sum_{k=1}^{M_{ij}} \left(T_{ijk}^0 + T_{ijk}^1 \right) \left(C_{ijk}^0 - C_{ijk}^1 \right)$$

where M_{ij} denotes the number of modes available for the group under analysis, for a trip from zone i to zone j. Nothing essential is lost with the simpler treatment given in the text.

where
N_{im} = number of trips on link i by mode m,
C_{im} = cost of traveling along link i by mode m,
K = set of links in the base network,
L = set of links in the modified network,
M = number of modes available for the group under analysis.

A graphical analysis of expression (3.7) is somewhat complicated. Jara-Díaz and Friesz (1982) developed a method to obtain modal demands from aggregated trip demand between a certain O-D pair, imposing the condition that perceived costs of all modes such that $T_{ijm} > 0$, are equal. They showed unambiguously how modal demand curves must shift, given a set of cost changes. The simple case of two substitutable modes between a certain O-D pair is illustrated in Figure 3.2, where a reduction in mode 1's perceived costs takes place (aggregate and modal supply curves are omitted in this figure).

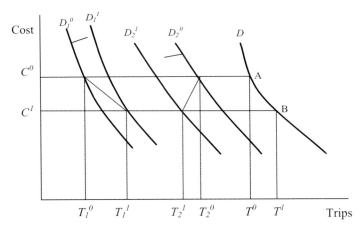

D = aggregate demand; D_i^t = modal demand for mode i at time t.
Figure 3.2. *Graphical interpretation of the rule-of-a-half for two competing modes.*

All of these developments and reasoning contribute to give a sounder theoretical base to *RH*, but it still retains most of the intuitive base of its beginnings. Williams (1976) brought strictness to the derivation. Starting from Hotelling's integral (3.2), Williams derived strictly the expression of the rule-of-a-half, clearly stating the assumptions behind it. In the one mode - several zones case, ΔMCS integrability conditions (3.3) may be expressed as:

$$\frac{\partial T_{ij}}{\partial C_{kl}} = \frac{\partial T_{kl}}{\partial C_{ij}} \qquad (3.8)$$

Provided such conditions hold, one can arbitrarily choose an integration path, because the value of Hotelling's integral would be path independent. A linear path from C^0 to C^1 can be parametrically defined as

$$L(\sigma) = \left(l_{ii}(\sigma), \dots, l_{ij}(\sigma), \dots, l_{nn}(\sigma) \right) \tag{3.9}$$

$$l_{ij}(\sigma) = C_{ij}^0 + \sigma\left(C_{ij}^1 - C_{ij}^0 \right) \tag{3.10}$$

$$L(\sigma = 0) = \left(C_{11}^0, \dots, C_{ij}^0, \dots C_{nn}^0 \right) = C^0 \tag{3.11}$$

$$L(\sigma = 1) = \left(C_{11}^1, \dots, C_{ij}^1, \dots C_{nn}^1 \right) = C^1 \tag{3.12}$$

Trip demand from zone i to zone j depends upon all interzonal costs, $(C_{11}, \dots, C_{nn})$ both before and after the cost changes:

$$T_{ij} = T_{ij}\left(C_{11}, \dots, C_{ij}, \dots C_{nn} \right) \tag{3.13}$$

Hotelling's integral can be written as:

$$\Delta MCS = -\int_{C^0}^{C^1} \sum_{i=1}^{n} \sum_{j=1}^{n} T_{ij}\left(C_{11}, \dots, C_{ij}, \dots C_{nn} \right) dC_{ij} \tag{3.14}$$

or, changing variables,

$$\Delta MCS = -\int_{\sigma=0}^{\sigma=1} \sum_{i=1}^{n} \sum_{j=1}^{n} T_{ij}\left(l_{ii}(\sigma), \dots, l_{ij}(\sigma), \dots, l_{nn}(\sigma) \right) \frac{dl_{ij}(\sigma)}{d\sigma} d\sigma \tag{3.15}$$

This becomes a summation of simple integrals. Calling $T_{ij}(L(\sigma)) = T_{ij}(\sigma)$ and considering that $\dfrac{dl_{ij}(\sigma)}{d\sigma} = C_{ij}^1 - C_{ij}^0$, it should be noted that equation (3.15) is an intermediate result that can be used to actually calculate any line integral representing ΔMCS using a linear path for known demand functions, provided condition (3.8) hold. Expanding $T_{ij}(\sigma)$ in a Taylor series around $\sigma = 0$, equation (3.15) becomes:

$$\Delta MCS = \sum_{i=1}^{n} \sum_{j=1}^{n} \left(C_{ij}^0 - C_{ij}^1 \right) \int_{\sigma=0}^{\sigma=1} \left[T_{ij}(\sigma = 0) + \sigma \frac{dT_{ij}}{d\sigma}\bigg|_{\sigma=0} + \frac{1}{2}\sigma^2 \frac{d^2 T_{ij}}{d\sigma^2}\bigg|_{\sigma=0} + \dots \right] d\sigma \tag{3.16}$$

Neglecting terms of second and higher order, which account for curvature effects in $T_{ij}(\sigma)$, and approximating $\left(dT_{ij}/d\sigma \right)_{\sigma=0}$ by $\left(T_{ij}^1 - T_{ij}^0 \right)$ where $T_{ij}^0 = T_{ij}(\sigma = 0)$, the final result is obtained:

$$\Delta MCS = \sum_{i=1}^{n}\sum_{j=1}^{n}\left(C_{ij}^{0}-C_{ij}^{1}\right)T_{ij}^{0}+\frac{1}{2}\sum_{i=1}^{n}\sum_{j=1}^{n}\left(C_{ij}^{0}+C_{ij}^{1}\right)\left(T_{ij}^{1}-T_{ij}^{0}\right) \qquad (3.17)$$

$$\Delta MCS =\frac{1}{2}\sum_{i=1}^{n}\sum_{j=1}^{n}\left(T_{ij}^{0}+T_{ij}^{1}\right)\left(C_{ij}^{0}-C_{ij}^{1}\right) \qquad (3.18)$$

Expression (3.18) is the rule-of-a-half for one mode of travel and several zones, deduced rigorously from Hotelling's integral. But it is important to recall that three assumptions were made:

(a)   integrability conditions hold;
(b)   series expansion of the function $T_{ij}(\sigma)$ around $\sigma=0$, neglecting terms of second and higher order; and
(c)   approximation $\left(dT_{ij}/d\sigma\right)\big|_{\sigma=0}$ by $\left(T_{ij}^{1}-T_{ij}^{0}\right)$

These two latter conditions indicate explicitly what we have already mentioned, namely, *RH* is favored as a good approximation of Marshallian users' benefits in absence of second (or higher) order effects of fares on demand, and under small variations of fares or perceived users' costs.

In summary, the rule-of-the-half can be seen as a simple and operational tool to assess Marshallian users' benefits. It can be applied even without knowledge about the underlying demand functions, since the only information required to perform the calculations is contained in the set of variables that describe market equilibrium with and without the project. But this property arises only as the nice face of the coin since first derivatives of market demands had to be assumed constant. Example 3.1 uses *RH* to approximate ΔMCS and also shows its limitations.

The most important limitation of *RH*, however, is that it represents an approximation of the Marshallian surplus, a measure that although may seem right, is actually quite arbitrary when we take a second look at its definition: *'The excess of the price which [the consumer] would be willing to pay rather than go without the thing, over that which he actually does pay'* might sound reasonable as a benefit measure, but certainly is purely a statement. How consistent is it with economic theory?

If we are interested in a rigorous user benefit measure derived from the general economic theory of utility maximization, it would be far from evident that Marshall's measure (and consequently the rule-of-the-half as well) should be the correct choice. To fully understand the limitations and biases hidden in ΔMCS and *RH*, we must return to economics foundations. But first let us present some examples of ΔMCS and *RH*.

Example 3.1. Using *RH* to approximate ΔMCS
Let us consider the demand function for car trips to work reported in Thomson (1974). The demand model is

$$T_a = 50118.72(C_a - 50)^{-1.66}$$ (3.19)

where C_a represents a cost (price) index that was created to take into account differences in distances and routes, in order to explain the total number of trips using car, T_a.

From (3.1), the exact value of ΔMCS can be easily shown to be

$$\Delta MCS = 75937.46 \left[(C_a^1 - 50)^{-0.66} - (C_a^0 - 50)^{-0.66} \right]$$ (3.20)

The demand model indicates that cost indices of 200, 100 and 80 generate approximately 12, 76 and 177 car trips respectively. For a drop of C_a from, say, 200 to 100, equation (3.20) gives us 2962 units of benefits, while RH, through equation (3.6), yields

$$RH = \tfrac{1}{2}(12.24 + 75.81)(200 - 100) = 4402 \text{ [units of benefits]}$$ (3.21)

which is clearly a gross overestimation of ΔMCS. However, when C_a drops from 100 to 80 (which increases demand in a greater number) RH gives a figure of 2528; not bad if we consider the exact value of ΔMCS being 2303. Evidently, RH does not approximate ΔMCS correctly in the first case because demand function (3.19) is extremely convex at low ranges, but it does approximate well in the second case since the function is nearly a straight line in the medium range. In other words, the second case fulfils two important conditions for RH to be a good approximation of users' benefits: small curvature of demand and little variation of perceived cost.

Example 3.2. ΔMCS for Logit: The Logsum formula
Let V_i be mode i's utility, as in definition Definition 2.1.The usual treatment of discrete choice mode analysis assumes that V_i cannot be known with certainty, and should be expressed as the sum of a function U_i of observed variables as the cost C_i and other qualities $\{q_{ji}\}$, and a random error E_i. Therefore, the probability p_b of choosing mode b is

$$\pi_b = P(U_b + E_b > U_i + E_i, \ \forall i \neq b)$$ (3.22)

What is a probability at an individual level is a proportion of the population with similar characteristics and perceptions (i.e. with the same utility function), so if the size of that population is N, then demand for trips T_i equals Np_i. Now let us take the popular Logit model to describe modal shares in this market –which is a particular choice for the probabilistic distribution of error terms-, which leads to

$$\pi_i = \frac{\exp(U_i)}{\displaystyle\sum_{j=1}^{M} \exp(U_j)}$$ (3.23)

Note that in this case, as in all modal split models, a given O-D pair is under analysis and welfare variations come from the change in individual modal choices following price and/or quality variations in one or more modes. Then, if one applies Williams' linear path procedure, checking integrability conditions should be made at a cross-mode level. Then it is quite easy to verify that for the typical U_i specification (i.e. linear in C_i and in each element of $\{q_{ji}\}$),

$$\frac{\partial T_i}{\partial C_j} = -N\theta\pi_i\pi_j = \frac{\partial T_j}{\partial C_i} \qquad (3.24)$$

where θ is the coefficient of mode cost. Equation (3.24) means integrability conditions hold, so ΔMCS has a unique value. Applying equation (3.15) and recalling that $-\theta$ equals the marginal utility of income, λ, one gets (Williams, 1977; Sasaki 1982)

$$\Delta MCS = \frac{N}{\lambda}\ln\sum_{i=1}^{M}\exp U_i\Big|_{C^0}^{C^1} \qquad (3.25)$$

The logarithm of the sum of utilities' exponentials is known as the logsum formula, which appears as a fairly well-funded form of valuing users' benefits from Logit modal choice models. We will return to this later in this chapter.

Example 3.3. ΔMCS for Entropy models
Transport demand models evolved enormously since the end of the sixties, particularly in urban studies. After a whole family of more or less *ad hoc* gravity type models, the idea of entropy acquired a respectable status as the most distinguished member of that family. The entropy approach appears to be a powerful method to overcome microscopic complexities when only aggregate data is available, although it is important to note that the entropy concept can be applied in a disaggregate framework as well (see Anas 1983).

It is well known (see, for example, Wilson 1967) that the model is derived from maximizing

$$F = -\sum_{ij} T_{ij}\ln T_{ij} \qquad (3.26)$$

subject to $$\sum_{ij} C_{ij}T_{ij} = C \qquad (3.27)$$

$$T_{ij} > 0 \qquad (3.28)$$

where T_{ij} denote trips from zone i to j, C_{ij} are the corresponding costs and C is the total cost. Depending on the available information, several constraints can be imposed to the maximization problem:

$$\sum_j T_{ij} = O_i \qquad (3.29)$$

$$\sum_i T_{ij} = D_j \tag{3.30}$$

If the general problem is solved, using all constraints (although non-negativity constraints prove to be unnecessary once constraints (3.29) and (3.30) are introduced), the solution in terms of Lagrangian multipliers (dual variables) takes the form:

$$T_{ij} = O_i D_j \exp-(\alpha_i + \gamma_j + \phi C_{ij}) \tag{3.31}$$

where ϕ, $\{\alpha_i\}$ and $\{\gamma_i\}$ are the Lagrangian multipliers associated with constraints (3.27), (3.29) and (3.30) respectively. It should be noted equation (3.31) looks like a demand function where trips depend on (the generalized) cost and ϕ plays the role of a cost coefficient. It is easy to show that the dual of this problem may be written as the unconstrained minimization problem over the dual variables $\{\alpha_i\}$, $\{\gamma_i\}$ and ϕ:

$$Min\, Z = \sum_{ij} O_i D_j \exp-(\alpha_i + \gamma_j + \phi C_{ij}) + \sum_i \alpha_i O_i + \sum_j \gamma_j D_j + \phi C \tag{3.32}$$

If it is assumed that ϕ does not depend on the interzonal trip costs $\{C_{ij}\}$, as is usually done, first order conditions on the dual lead to:

$$\frac{\partial Z}{\partial C_{ij}} = -\phi T_{ij} + \phi \frac{\partial C}{\partial C_{ij}} \tag{3.33}$$

where T_{ij} is the primal solution expressed in terms of the dual variables, as in equation (3.31). From (3.33), T_{ij} can be rewritten as

$$T_{ij} = \frac{\partial C}{\partial C_{ij}} - \frac{1}{\phi}\frac{\partial Z}{\partial C_{ij}} \tag{3.34}$$

Deriving T_{ij} with respect to an arbitrary C_{kl}:

$$\frac{\partial T_{ij}}{\partial C_{kl}} = \frac{\partial^2 C}{\partial C_{kl}\partial C_{ij}} - \frac{1}{\phi}\frac{\partial^2 Z}{\partial C_{kl}\partial C_{ij}} \tag{3.35}$$

With the assumption made of $\partial\phi/\partial C_{ij} = 0$, $\forall i, j$, integrability conditions, i.e. $(\partial T_{ij}/\partial C_{kl}) = (\partial T_{kl}/\partial C_{ij})$, are satisfied, so that ΔMCS can be evaluated using Hotelling's line integral between two cost situations C^0 and C^1. Replacing T_{ij} by equation (3.34)

$$\Delta MCS = \int_{C^0}^{C^1} \sum_{ij} \left(\frac{1}{\phi}\frac{\partial Z}{\partial C_{ij}} - \frac{\partial C}{\partial C_{ij}} \right) dC_{ij} \tag{3.36}$$

$$\Delta MCS = \int_{C^0}^{C^1} \left(\frac{1}{\phi} \sum_{ij} \frac{\partial Z}{\partial C_{ij}} dC_{ij} - \sum_{ij} \frac{\partial C}{\partial C_{ij}} dC_{ij} \right) \tag{3.37}$$

$$\Delta MCS = \int_{Z^0}^{Z^1} \frac{1}{\phi} dZ - \int_{C^0}^{C^1} dC \tag{3.38}$$

$$\Delta MCS = \frac{1}{\phi} \left(Z^1 - Z^0 \right) - \left(C^1 - C^0 \right) \tag{3.39}$$

But optimum values of primal and dual problems must coincide, so (3.39) may also be expressed as (Williams, 1976)

$$\Delta MCS = \frac{1}{\phi} \left(F^1 - F^0 \right) - \left(C^1 - C^0 \right) \tag{3.40}$$

Expression (3.40) links the entropy concept with consumers' surplus, assuming that the dual variable ϕ does not depend on costs $\{C_{ij}\}$. Using equations (3.26) and (3.31) this result can be given an alternative expression linking ΔMCS with benefits in origins and destinations. Note the preceding result can be extended to a distribution-modal split framework, basically keeping the same ana lytical properties in relation to welfare measures.

3.3. Back to the drawing board

3.3.1. The neo-classical approach: Basics

It is now time to depart from the intuitive grounds where Marshall's measure and the rule-of-a-half were born, and explore users' benefits beginning at the foundations of the neo-classical economic theory in order to determine rigorous measures to asses them. To do it, let us begin with a general formulation and some basic properties.

Starting from the optimization problem that is assumed to represent consumers' behavior in the neoclassical theory (*Problem A* below), and using the (so-called) dual of this problem (*Problem B* below), three different ways of assigning money measures to variations of utility are derived given a general variation of the price vector.[10]

The following notation will be used at an individual or household level:

$X = \{Xi\}$, vector of goods and services consumed in a period.
$U = U(X)$, utility function.

---

[10] The mathematical properties and conditions that have to be fulfilled by the economic functions appearing in this section, are not listed unless strictly necessary for welfare analysis. For a full description of such properties, Varian (1978) and Malinvaud (1969) are good references.

$P = \{Pi\}$, vector of prices of goods and services.
I = personal (or household) income.

The following problem and its solution represent consumer behavior:

Problem A

$$MaxU(X)$$

subject to: $$\sum_i P_i X_i \leq I$$

$$X_i \geq 0$$

Solution: $X = X^*(P,I)$, demand functions.
Optimum: $U[X^*(P, I)] = V(P, I)$, indirect utility function.

Problem A states that, given prices and income, a person searches for a bundle of goods and services which maximizes its utility as he or she perceives it. The amount the individual prefers depends on prices of all goods and income: a demand function. The maximum utility he or she can reach is the one which corresponds to the preferred bundle, thus indirectly dependant on prices and income. This *indirect utility function* will be shown extremely useful when defining welfare measures.

A second problem, which is said to be dual to A, leads to interesting results.

Problem B

$$Min \sum_i P_i X_i$$

subject to: $$U(X) \geq \overline{U}$$

$$X_i \geq 0$$

Solution: $X = X^c(P,\overline{U})$, compensated demand
Optimum: $PX^c(P,\overline{U}) = e(P,\overline{U})$, expenditure function.

Here, utility level is given and the wanted bundle X is the one which requires the minimum expenditure. Optimal quantities now depend on prices and on the utility level previously set as minimally acceptable. Therefore, the minimal necessary expenditure is a function of prices and utility.

The relation between *Problems A and B* is presented graphically in Figure 3.3. From this, it is clear that the inverse of $U = V(P, I)$ in I is precisely $I = e(P, U)$.

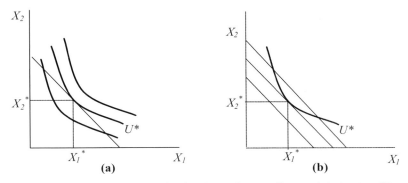

Figure 3.3. *Utility maximization (a) and expenditure minimization (b)*

Property 3.1: Derivative of expenditure function
Using a basic property of optimization problems, it can be shown that[11]

$$\frac{\partial e(P,U)}{\partial P_i} = X_i^c(P,U)$$ (3.41)

Property 3.2: Basic identities
Identities (3.42) to (3.45) follow from *Problems A* and *B*.

- The maximum utility an individual can reach with an income equal to the minimum necessary to reach a level U at given prices, is precisely U, i.e.

$$V[P, e(P, U)] \equiv U$$ (3.42)

- The minimum expenditure necessary to reach the maximum utility an individual can reach with an income equal to I, is precisely I, i.e.

$$e[P, V(P, I)] \equiv I$$ (3.43)

- The market demand with an income equal to the minimum necessary to reach a level U at given prices is equal to the compensated demand at the same level U, i.e.

$$X_i[P, e(P,U)] \equiv X_i^c(P,U)$$ (3.44)

- The compensated demand at the maximum utility an individual can reach with an income I, is equal to the market demand with the same income I, i.e.

---

[11] A non strict proof is given in Diamond and McFadden (1974), where other properties of the expenditure function are also explained. A strict derivation can be made applying the envelope theorem.

$$X_i^C\left[P,V(P,I)\right] \equiv X_i(P,I) \tag{3.45}$$

On the other hand, differentiating both sides of identity (3.42) with respect to P_i yields

$$\frac{\partial V}{\partial P_i} + \frac{\partial V}{\partial I}\frac{\partial e}{\partial P_i} = 0 \tag{3.46}$$

and using (3.41) and (3.45) we get,

Property 3.3: Roy's identity

$$X_i = -\frac{\partial V/\partial P_i}{\partial V/\partial I} \tag{3.47}$$

Now, differentiating both sides of identity (3.45) with respect to P_j yields

$$\frac{\partial X_i}{\partial P_j} + \frac{\partial X_i}{\partial I}\frac{\partial e}{\partial P_j} = \frac{\partial X_i^C}{\partial P_j} \tag{3.48}$$

and using (3.41) and (3.45) again, the following equation emerges:

Property 3.4: Slutsky Equation

$$\frac{\partial X_i}{\partial P_j} = \frac{\partial X_i^C}{\partial P_j} - X_j(P,I)\frac{\partial X_i}{\partial I} \tag{3.49}$$

This property provides the link between compensated demands and market demands, showing that the effect of a price change on Marshallian demands has two components: the change in the compensated demand due to the price change (the substitution effect) and the change in the Marshallian demand due to an income change (the income effect).

These are all the necessary tools we need to search for rigorous measures of users' benefits.

3.3.2. The compensating and equivalent variations

If the set of prices changes from P^0 to P^1, the bundle of goods consumed changes from X^0 to X^1, and the level of utility varies from U_0 to U_1. Money spent is the same, but utility differs. How can the difference $U_1 - U_0$ be measured in monetary terms? Hicks (1956) gave two strict answers to this question.

Definition 3.2 : Equivalent variation
The equivalent variation, *EV*, is defined as the change in income that provokes the same effect on *utility* as the price change. That is,

$$U_1 = V\left(P^1,I\right) = V\left(P^0,\ I+EV\right) \tag{3.50}$$

It is useful to show the relation between *EV* and demand. This can be done making use of the expenditure function Taking the inverse in equation (3.50),

$$I = e\left(P^{1}, U_{1}\right) \text{ and } I + EV = e\left(P^{0}, U_{1}\right) \tag{3.51}$$

Therefore,

$$EV = e\left(P^{0}, U_{1}\right) - e\left(P^{1}, U_{1}\right) \tag{3.52}$$

For *U* constant, the differential of *e(P,U)* is

$$de(P, U) = \sum_{i} \frac{\partial e}{\partial P_{i}} dP_{i} \tag{3.53}$$

Finally, using equation (3.41) and noting (3.52) can be obtained integrating (3.53), we get

$$EV = -\int_{P0}^{P1} \sum_{i} X_{i}^{c}(P, U_{1}) dPi \tag{3.54}$$

This shows *EV* can be interpreted graphically as the sum of areas to the left of compensated demands with utility held constant at the level of U_1, as illustrated in Figure 3.4.

Definition 3.3: Compensating variation
The second Hicksian answer is the compensating variation, *CV*, which is the change in income that exactly offsets the effect of the price variation on utility, i.e.

$$U_{0} = V\left(P^{0}, I\right) = V\left(P^{1}, I - CV\right) \tag{3.55}$$

such that *CV* is positive if prices diminish.

Following the same procedure as before,

$$I = e\left(P^{0}, U_{0}\right) \text{ and } I - CV = e\left(P^{1}, U_{0}\right) \tag{3.56}$$

$$CV = e\left(P^{0}, U_{0}\right) - e\left(P^{1}, U_{0}\right) \tag{3.57}$$

$$CV = -\int_{P0}^{P1} \sum_{i} X_{i}^{c}(P, U_{0}) dPi \tag{3.58}$$

As *EV*, graphically *CV* is also the sum of areas to the left of compensated demands, but at a different utility level (U_0), as shown in Figure 3.4. This figure is helpful to see *EV* and *CV* have different values, a fact that may make us wonder which one should be preferred. The literature offers a straightforward answer: either one is equally acceptable, as long as we choose a set of prices as reference (prices before or after the change) and then use our chosen measure consistently.

Have we found what we were looking for? Both *EV* and *CV* are unambiguous income-like equivalents to utility changes and the problem seems to be solved. Unfortunately, it is not; at least, not exactly. Neither utility nor compensated demands can be observed. Thus, equations (3.50), (3.54), (3.55) or (3.58) seem only to be nice but useless constructions, unlikely to be of any help in practice. Whether this is true or not will be looked at next.

3.3.3. Linking consumer's surplus with equivalent and compensating variations

It is interesting to note that *EV*, *CV* and *ΔMCS* are all expressed in the form of a line integral. But although *ΔMCS* integral depends on the integration path, that is not the case for *EV* and *CV* integrals, since at any level of utility,

$$\frac{\partial X_i^c(P,U)}{\partial P_j} = \frac{\partial(\partial e/\partial P_i)}{\partial P_j} = \frac{\partial^2 e}{\partial P_i \partial P_j} = \frac{\partial(\partial e/\partial P_j)}{\partial P_i} = \frac{\partial X_j^c(P,U)}{\partial P_i} \tag{3.59}$$

which indicates the result is unique in each case.

If only one price changes, *EV*, *CV* and *ΔMCS* can be easily represented graphically as in Figure 3.4 (for a price reduction). From this, the Marshallian measure appears to be "in between" the Hicksian ones. This could be surprising if one recalls that, unlike the former, these latter are rigorous money equivalents of utility variation.

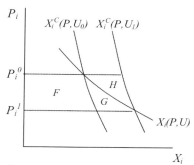

Figure 3.4 : The relation between demand and money measures of utility variation after one price reduction. EV= F + G + H; CV= F; ΔMCS = F + G.

Roy's identity (see equation (3.47)) is very helpful to clarify the relation between Marshall's measure and Hick's measures: replacing it in equation (3.2) and assuming $\partial V/\partial I$ is constant (constant marginal utility of income) and equal to λ, we get

$$\Delta MCS = \int_{P^0}^{P^1} \sum_i \frac{\partial V/\partial P_i}{\partial V/\partial I}\, dP_i = \frac{1}{\lambda}\int_{P^0}^{P^1} \sum_i \frac{\partial V}{\partial Pi}\, dP_i = \frac{1}{\lambda}\int_{V^0}^{V^1} dV \qquad (3.60)$$

therefore, ΔMCS becomes

$$\Delta MCS = \frac{1}{\lambda}\left[V(P^1,I) - V(P^0,I)\right] \qquad (3.61)$$

This expression clearly shows that ΔMCS has a direct relation with utility variation. Undoubtedly, equation (3.61) provides ΔMCS with a more solid defense than the pure intuition it was originally built from. Moreover, it is a relation that tolerates changes in all prices and is path independent, as EV and CV. However, equation (3.61) was generated assuming constancy of the marginal utility of income between P^0 and P^1. This is related with two assumptions that went nearly unnoticed when deriving ΔMCS for both the entropy and Logit models: constancy of the generalized interzonal cost coefficient ϕ in equation (3.33) and linearity of modal utility in equation (3.24). In both cases, integrability conditions depended on that fact, something that is now connected with equation (3.61).

In this sense, then, ΔMCS is less strict than EV and CV as a money measure of ordinal preferences[12]. Willig (1976) set bounds to the difference (percentage) between ΔMCS and each of the 'sane' measures EV and CV, showing that the relative error is given by $\eta \Delta MCS/2I$, where η is the income elasticity of demand. **This shows that ΔMCS may be a good approximation of a rigorous benefit measure, provided price variations are small and the consumption of the corresponding goods and services are relatively insensitive to income level.** This should be no surprise, as equations (3.2), (3.54) and (3.58) are identical in form but relate to different demand concepts, and the Slutsky equation (3.49) shows that the absence of income effect makes the effect of prices on Hicksian and Marshallian demands equal.

So EV and CV are linked with ΔMCS. And the latter can be seen, under certain conditions, as a proxy for the former. Yet, EV and CV do not have a simple, straight forward form one can use to estimate them, at least not as easily as it is with ΔMCS, so in many occasions it is reasonable to settle for ΔMCS, understanding its limitations. If one is interested in EV and CV, however, then some additional work will be necessary. A possibility is to use estimated market demands and then use Roy's identity as a differential equation to find an indirect utility function V, a procedure proposed by Hausman (1981). Once V (or part of it) has been found, the expenditure function can be obtained, from which CV and EV can be derived. Another very interesting possibility is exploiting the Slutsky equation, a procedure we will explore soon. First, let us take a look at CV and EV when it is not prices that change, but qualities of certain goods, like transport mode's characteristics.

---

[12] For a good discussion on the relation among money measures of utility, ordinality and cardinality of preferences, see Morey (1984).

3.3.4. Users' benefits from qualitative changes

A variation in utility can occur not only because of a price change but also due to quality variations. This justifies the expansion of the concept behind CV (or EV) to include such changes. This is particularly useful within the framework of discrete choices where qualitative dimensions of alternatives are explicitly used in the indirect utility function, as seen in Chapter 2.

Assuming the marginal utility of income λ to be independent of prices and qualities of modes, and assuming transport expenses to be unimportant in the total consumer's budget (negligible income effect), as is typically made, Small and Rosen (1981) carefully showed that CV after a change of transport prices or qualities which induce individual welfare changes from U_i^0 to U_i^1, is given by

$$CV = \frac{N}{\lambda} \int_{U^0}^{U^1} \sum_{i=1}^{M} \pi_i \left(U_1, ... U_M \right) dU_i \qquad (3.62)$$

In the case of the Logit formulation, this result gives us a generalized version of the logsum formula already presented, i.e.

$$CV = \frac{N}{\lambda} \ln \sum_{i=1}^{M} \exp U_i \Big|_{U^0}^{U^1} \qquad (3.63)$$

That this is a consistent measure of welfare can also be seen from its property as the expected maximum utility at any given level of a utility tree. Then the logsum acts as the representative utility or composite cost when moving one level up in the (hierarchical) Logit formulation. That makes it very easy to extend the result to a framework of mode-destination choice (Williams, 1977; Sasaki 1982).

Now, starting from equation (3.62) we can deduce another interesting result obtained by Jara-Díaz (1990). Choosing a linear path of integration and letting

$$U_i = U_i^0 + \theta \left(U_i^1 - U_i^0 \right) \qquad (3.64)$$

then $U_i(0) = U_i^0$, $U_i(1) = U_i^1$ and $dU_i = \Delta U_i d\theta$, where $\Delta U_i = U_i^1 - U_i^0$. Changing variables we get:

$$CV = \frac{N}{\lambda} \int_0^1 \sum_{i=1}^{M} \pi_i \left[U_1(\theta), ... U_M(\theta) \right] \Delta U_i d\theta = \frac{N}{\lambda} \sum_{i=1}^{M} \Delta U_i \int_0^1 \pi_i \left[U_1(\theta), ... U_M(\theta) \right] d\theta \quad (3.65)$$

The line integral has been reduced to a sum of simple integrals. If we further assume linearity of π_i between the 0 and 1 states, $\forall i$, we finally get the compact form

$$CV = \frac{N}{\lambda} \sum_{i=1}^{M} \Delta U_i \bar{\pi}_i = \frac{1}{\lambda} \sum_{i=1}^{M} \Delta U_i \bar{T}_i \qquad (3.66)$$

with $\bar{\pi}_i$ defined as $\frac{1}{2}\left(\pi_i^0 + \pi_i^1\right)$; $\bar{T}_i = N\bar{\pi}_i$ is the expected number of mode i's users.

Let us now turn our attention to the arguments of U_i, which we will define as
C_i : user money cost of a trip by mode i, as before,
q_{hi} : mode i's quality dimension h (e.g., minus travel time).

Then a local variation in utility, ΔU_i, can be expressed in terms of local variations of cost and quality (ΔC_i and Δq_{hi} respectively), i.e.

$$\Delta U_i = \frac{\partial U_i}{\partial C_i} \Delta C_i + \sum_h \frac{\partial U_i}{\partial q_{hi}} \Delta q_{hi} \qquad (3.67)$$

Replacing (3.67) in (3.66) we obtain

$$CV = \sum_i \frac{\partial U_i / \partial C_i}{\lambda} \Delta C_i \bar{T}_i + \sum_i \sum_h \frac{\partial U_i / \partial q_{hi}}{\lambda} \Delta q_{hi} \bar{T}_i \qquad (3.68)$$

Here we have to recall some basic definitions and microeconomic properties of discrete choice theory (Chapter 2). First of all, the marginal utility of income is equal to minus the partial derivative of the (conditional indirect) utility function with respect to cost (Definition 2.2), i.e.

$$-\frac{\partial U_i / \partial C_i}{\lambda} = 1 \qquad (3.69)$$

On the other hand, the implicit trade-off between cost and quality dimension h at a constant level of utility is the subjective value of h, SV_h (Definition 2.3)

$$SV_h = \frac{\partial U_i / \partial q_{hi}}{\lambda} \qquad (3.70)$$

Replacing (3.69) and (3.70) in equation (3.68) and after elementary manipulations, we finally obtain the main result:

$$CV = -\sum_i \Delta C_i \bar{T}_i + \sum_h SV_h \sum_i \bar{T}_i \Delta q_{hi} \qquad (3.71)$$

Equation (3.71) shows the welfare measure (3.62) is approximately equal to the rule-of-a-half measure after a price change, plus a series of terms induced by quality variations, each one weighted by its corresponding subjective value. So this may be seen as a generalized version of the rule-of-a-half, where benefits come not only from changes in prices but in modes' characteristics as well. Note that this result coincides with the approximation of ΔMCS given in equation (3.18) when there are no quality changes. This should be no surprise as λ has been assumed constant, which was the condition for ΔMCS to be a right measure of welfare change (equation (3.61)).

Do note that result (3.71) can be obtained if C_i in equation (3.18) is defined as the money cost plus the "costs" imposed by the mode's qualities (i.e. their values multiplied by their associated subjective values). With C_i built that way, "cost" would then be interpreted as a more general description of the mode's advantages/disadvantages; a *generalized cost of mode i*. And therefore, our result (3.71) is not only a more complete version of the rule-of-a-half, but can be seen as a consequence of sophisticating the concept of "cost".

3.3.5. Income effect in the estimation of users' benefits

To finish our journey across user benefit measures, we should pay some attention now to an assumption we had to make a few times: considering marginal utility of income as a constant within the range of price (and/or quality) changes. Normally that is considered a reasonable assumption for developed countries, but it is certainly not so in developing ones, where expenses in transport are a rather important fraction of many socio-economic groups' budget.

What happens if we choose not to ignore this "income effect"? Following the expression for the compensating variation found in (3.57), the expenditure function $e(P^1, U_0)$ can be approximated through a second order Taylor expansion from $e(P^0, U_0)$, that is,

$$e(P^1, U_0) \cong e(P^0, U_0) + \sum_i \left. \frac{\partial e(P, U_0)}{\partial P_i} \right|_{P_0} \Delta P_i + \tfrac{1}{2} \sum_i \sum_j \left. \frac{\partial^2 e(P, U_0)}{\partial P_i \partial P_j} \right|_{P_0} \Delta P_i \Delta P_j \quad (3.72)$$

where $\Delta P_i = P_i^1 - P_i^0$. Using the derivative property (3.41), we get from equations (3.57) and (3.72),

$$CV \cong -\sum_i \left. X_i^C (P, U_0) \right|_{P_0} \Delta P_i - \tfrac{1}{2} \sum_i \sum_j \left. \frac{\partial X_j^C (P, U_0)}{\partial P_i} \right|_{P_0} \Delta P_i \Delta P_j \quad (3.73)$$

Solving the Slutsky equation (3.49) for $\partial X_j^C / \partial P_i$, replacing in (3.73) and noting that $X_i^C (P^0, U_0) = X_i (P^0, I_0)$ (from (3.45) with $U = V(P, I)$), we get

$$CV \cong -\sum_i X_i (P^0, I_0) \Delta P_i - \tfrac{1}{2} \sum_i \sum_j \left. \frac{\partial X_j (P, I_0)}{\partial P_i} \right|_{P_0} \Delta P_i \Delta P_j - \tfrac{1}{2} \sum_i \sum_j \left. \frac{\partial X_j (P^0, I)}{\partial I} \right|_{I_0} X_i (P^0, I_0) \Delta P_i \Delta P_j \quad (3.74)$$

Equation (3.74) is an approximation of the compensating variation after a price change, expressed only in terms of market demands, including income effect. Unlike compensated demands, market demands can be estimated and used to calculate *CV*. In this derivation, Slutsky equation plays a key role, since it provides the link between the (unobserved) compensated demands and the (observed) market demands.

Now we will show that the expression obtained for *CV* can be readily interpreted in terms of more traditional measures. To see this, the generalization of the Marshallian consumers' surplus variation shown in (3.2) will be considered, which would yield an exact measure of welfare if there were no income effect: It can be shown, by a simple expansion of demand about the initial price vector, that the first two terms of equation (3.74) represent an approximation of *ΔMCS* provided that second order effects of prices on demand are negligible and the Jacobian matrix of the vector of market demands, evaluated at P^0, is symmetrical (for a proof see Jara-Díaz and Videla, 1990). Thus, the approximated measure of *CV* has two components: the traditional welfare measure that would be used if income effect were not taken into account, and an **income-induced welfare impact** (*IWI*) given by the last terms in equation (3.74), that is,

$$CV \approx \Delta MCS - \frac{1}{2}\sum_i \sum_j \left. \frac{\partial X_j(P^0, I)}{\partial I}\right|_{I_0} X_i(P^0, I_0)\Delta P_i \Delta P_j = \Delta MCS + IWI \quad (3.75)$$

It should be noted that a similar result can be obtained for the equivalent variation *EV*, by simply expanding the expenditure function around (P^1, U_1). Note that *IWI* increases with the income elasticity of demand of those goods having a price change.

For synthesis, an intuitive measure like *ΔMCS* can be given a microeconomic foundation under conditions that are not too demanding, namely constancy of the marginal utility of income within the range of price variation. And if these conditions are not met, then the right measures, *CV* and *EV*, can be calculated using market demands.

3.4. Derived nature of transport demand and economic benefits

When viewing transport markets within the framework described in the preceding sections, the role of transport demand as the basis for the valuation of users' benefits becomes obvious: it succinctly provides the information on users' behavior, captured from actual observations which can be manipulated and converted into some monetary measure of utility. However, price variations in transport markets induce changes in supply and/or demand in several other economic activities. This is particularly clear when transport is viewed as a factor of production, i.e. as a service necessary both to bring inputs to and to deliver outputs from a particular plant. In the urban case this is also true, from a similar viewpoint, for trips with very different purposes: work, study, shopping, entertainment, etc. Then a fundamental question arises: **is it necessary to add potential benefits *induced* by improvements in the transport system on other economic activities?** Answers to this question have been given from different viewpoints in the literature. It is worth reviewing a couple of them.

Mishan (1976, pp. 79) warns against double counting when calculating benefits due to, for instance, the construction of a new railroad. *"...if this new railroad so reduces the time and increases the convenience of travel as to offer new job opportunities to a number of men, we ought not to include the measure of these new rents (a measure of the increase in their welfare from switching to the new jobs) as additional benefits. For such benefits are already subsumed in the (potential) consumers' surplus of the new railroad. Such a measure of consumers' surplus (approximated, say, by an estimate of the potential demand schedule for train journeys per annum) reveals the maximum sum each person will pay for a number of train journeys. And in determining this maximum sum, he will take into account the rents of the new jobs and, indeed, all other incidental utilities and disutilities accruing to him from the new railroad service".*

Similarly, Mohring (1976) analyses the cost reduction achievable by substituting transport for manufacturing inputs, following a reduction in unit transport cost. He shows that a consumers' surplus type measure in the firm's transport demand schedule accounts for all benefits accruing to the firm. In fact, Mohring's is a particular case of the general problem regarding the relation between factor and final goods markets treated by Carlton (1979) and, in a very strict form, by Jacobsen (1979).

In short, it appears that adding other benefits related to changes in the transport market would lead to double counting, so transport users' benefits should be the only measure to compute. The reason is simple: demanding transport only reflects a demand for something else; transport is simply a mean to overcome *distance*, a mean by which consumer and supplier -of whatever good or service we are analyzing- can find each other on the same spot. Consequently, the magnitude and shape of transport demand is basically an extension of the demand for other product/service, meaning the benefits one can measure in the transport market are no other than the benefits of consuming such product/service. Transport demand is *derived* from other demands.

This can be shown formally. Let us define two locations where an aggregate commodity is produced and consumed in a competitive environment, where Q_i is the amount of aggregate commodity produced at i and p_i is the price of aggregate commodity at i. The following relations are assumed:

$$Q_i = D_i(p_i) \quad \text{(demand at } i) \tag{3.76}$$

$$Q_i = S_i(p_i) \quad \text{(supply at } i) \tag{3.77}$$

Further, let us assume that the equilibrium price p_1^0 at market 1 is greater than at the market 2, p_2^0. With prices lower than p_1^0, consumers at 1 demand more than producers are willing to sell; the *excess demand* is given by

$$ED_1(p_1) = D_1(p_1) - S_1(p_1) \tag{3.78}$$

Similarly, with prices greater than p_2^0, producers at market 2 are willing to sell more than consumers want to buy; the *excess supply* is given by

$$ES_2(p_2) = S_2(p_2) - D_2(p_2) \tag{3.79}$$

Figure 3.5 (top) shows D_i, S_i, ED_1 and ES_2.

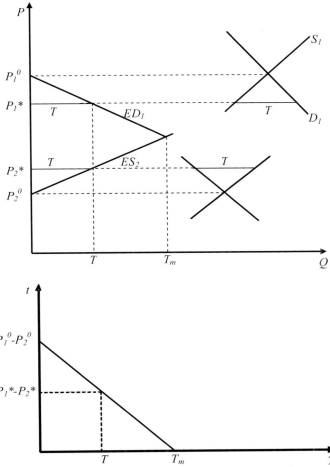

Figure 3.5: *Derivation of Transport Demand*

On the other hand, if a quantity T is produced in excess at market 2 and sold at market 1, then it has to hold that

$$T = ES_2(p_2) = ED_1(p_1) \tag{3.80}$$

If this amount T is brought from market 2 to 1, buyers would be paying prices $p_1{}^* < p_1{}^0$ and $p_2{}^* > p_2{}^0$ at markets 1 and 2, respectively, such that

$$p_1^{\ *} = ED_1^{\ -1}(T) \tag{3.81}$$

and

$$p_2^{\ *} = ES_2^{\ -1}(T) \tag{3.82}$$

which are also represented in Figure 3.5.

Thus, the willingness to pay for T units produced at market 2 and consumed at market 1 is p_1^*, or p_2^* plus the transport fare. In other words, the willingness to pay, t, for the movement of T units from 2 to 1 is given by

$$t = p_1^{\ *} - p_2^{\ *} = ED_1^{\ -1}(T) - ES_2^{\ -1}(T) = t(T) \tag{3.83}$$

which represents the transport demand, shown in Figure 3.5 (bottom).

Let us assume that transport supply is such that equilibrium takes place at $T=T_e$ and $t=t_e$. Transport consumers' surplus TCS is then given by

$$TCS = \int_0^{T_e} t(T)dT - t_e T_e \tag{3.84}$$

graphically represented in Figure 3.6 (top). Then, following equation (3.83), TCS is also given by

$$TCS = \int_0^{T_e} ED_1^{\ -1}(T)dT - \int_0^{T_e} ES_2^{\ -1}(T)dT - \left(p_1^1 - p_2^1\right)T_e \tag{3.85}$$

which can be rewritten as

$$TCS = \left[\int_0^{T_e} ED_1^{\ -1}(T)dT - p_1^1 T_e\right] + \left[p_2^1 T_e - \int_0^{T_e} ES_2^{\ -1}(T)dT\right]$$

or

$$TCS = \int_{p_1^1}^{p_1^0} ED_1(p_1)dp_1 + \int_{p_2^0}^{p_2^1} ES_2(p_2)dp_2 \tag{3.86}$$

represented by areas A and B, respectively, in Figure 3.6 (bottom). Finally, recalling equations (3.78) and (3.79)

$$TCS = -\int_{p_1^1}^{p_1^0} D_1(p_1)dp_1 + \int_{p_1^1}^{p_1^0} S_1(p_1)dp_1 + \int_{p_2^0}^{p_2^1} S_2(p_2)dp_2 - \int_{p_2^0}^{p_2^1} D_2(p_2)dp_2 \tag{3.87}$$

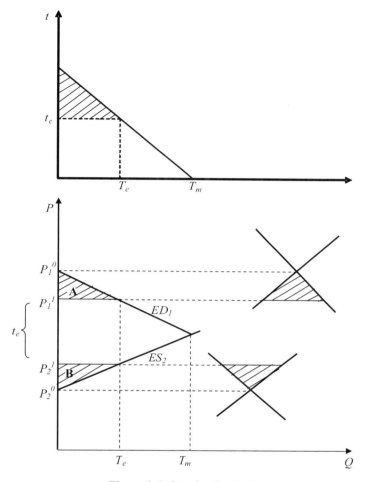

Figure 3.6: *Surplus Equivalences*

Thus, noting that S_i is the marginal cost curve of the industry if competition is assumed, *TCS* equals the algebraic sum of the variation in consumers' surplus (positive) and industry profits (negative) in market 1, plus the increase in profit in market 2 and the reduction in consumers' surplus in the same market. These net values are represented by the shaded quasi triangles regarding the local supply and demand curves in Figure 3.6 (bottom). Therefore, **under competition, transport consumers' surplus summarizes the welfare effects on consumers and producers of both markets.** This property continues to hold for variations in the transport market equilibrium due to, for instance, improvements in the link between markets 1 and 2. Jara-Díaz (1986) extended the analysis to monopolistic environments in related markets, showing that in this case transport consumers' surplus fails to reflect accurately the net sum of gains and losses of all producers and consumers, but can be considered an approximation whose precision depends on the degree of monopoly power at each location.

Note that our conclusion covers the land market as well; increased value of real state generated by a new transport project does not need to be accounted for separately, as it is already measured in transport demand.

3.5. Social benefits from transport projects

It does matter who pays for transport projects. If they are financed by users directly, then willingness to pay will determine which projects will be materialized and which will be postponed, while users' benefits measures like the ones we have seen can help us study changes in users' well being. But if projects are financed with tax money, things are not exactly the same. It should be clear from our analysis, both in this chapter and the preceding one, that what is behind transport demand –and therefore behind willingness to pay and users' benefits- is each individual's subjective perception of the value of his/her own time, own comfort, own safety, and so on. Such very personal valuation, however, may not be equal to the importance society as a whole gives to that person's well being. In other words, society's willingness to pay to improve someone's mobility conditions may differ from what he or she is willing to pay for such improvement.

Society has its own budget and its own priorities, and clearly total welfare is not necessarily the simple sum of all users' benefits. The fact that perceptions about the value of travel time savings and other variables vary among different groups in society, makes it evident that simply summing different groups' benefits –which is a particular form of aggregation- will lead to the overrepresentation of certain individuals; those whose valuation of their own time and comfort is higher (due to their low marginal utility of income, for example). Such situation may of course be acceptable and desirable if public policy is defined in such way, but certainly other forms of aggregation, reflecting other types of public preferences, are possible.

The following analysis focuses on the specific attribute of travel time, given its importance in the transport field, but it must be stressed that other attributes, and not only from the transport industry, can be looked at in an analogous way.

We should start then by introducing the **Social Price of Time (*SPT*)**, which opposes the personal version of the Subjective Value of Travel Time Savings (*SVTTS*) and represents the value society gives to a member's time. What can be said about the way society sees this variable? From the point of view of a society as a whole, reductions of an individual's travel time can be looked at positively for various reasons. One is the potential increase in actual wealth if such reductions translate into more work. Other is the increase in well-being, as this includes individual utility directly, which increases indeed as travel conditions improve. Under the approach that regards time as a productive resource only, the social price of time would be the value of the individual's marginal product of labor, if travel time reductions induce an equivalent amount of additional work. And if working time is unaltered by travel time changes, then *SPT* would be nil; this would be the case in pleasure trips or trips made during the leisure period, i.e. out of the (fixed) work schedule. But under the approach that views time as an element that influences individual utility, all gains should be accounted for, because they mean an increase in social welfare irrespective of changes in wealth.

In a perfectly competitive labor market, the wage rate would represent the value of the marginal productivity of labor. If we look at the original version of the goods-leisure model (in which neither work time nor travel time are in the direct utility function), then *SVTTS* is exactly given by the wage rate (see section 2.2.3). Thus, if this rate truly represents marginal productivity, then the subjective value of travel time would be equal to the social price and both would be equal to w, under the production approach. But under the welfare approach this would be different.

Following Pearce and Nash (1981), a social utility or welfare function can be used to represent the implicit preferences in the domain of public decisions. Such a function W_s has each person's utility level as arguments, and therefore it represents the way in which society takes into account individual (or group) welfare. Then

$$W_s = W_s\left(U_1,...U_q,...U_n\right)$$ (3.88)

If dB_q is the money equivalent of person q's variation in utility (consumer's surplus) due to a project, then social welfare would change by

$$dW_s = \sum_q \frac{dW_s}{dU_q}\frac{\partial U_q}{\partial I}dB_q$$ (3.89)

Following Gálvez and Jara-Díaz (1989), from equation (3.71) consumer's surplus variation for one individual after a travel time reduction Δt_q is approximately given by

$$dB_q = SVTTS_q \Delta t_q$$ (3.90)

As $\partial U_q/\partial I$ is the marginal utility of income λ_q, then

$$dW_s = \sum_q \Omega_q \lambda_q SVTTS_q \Delta t_q$$ (3.91)

where Ω_q is the social weight $\partial W_s/\partial U_q$. A factor λ_s is needed to convert dW_s into money. The tax system provides a socially-accepted equivalence between:

- the total welfare loss of those who pay taxes,

$$dW_s = \sum_q \frac{dW_s}{dU_q} \frac{\partial U_q}{\partial T_q} dT_q \tag{3.92}$$

where T_q is the tax paid by individual q

-and the total bill collected

$$dT = \sum_q dT_q \tag{3.93}$$

Definition 3.4: Social utility of money
The social utility of money is defined as

$$\lambda_s \equiv \frac{dW_s}{dT} \tag{3.94}$$

using (3.92)

$$\lambda_s = \sum_q \frac{dW_s}{dU_q} \frac{\partial U_q}{\partial T_q} \frac{dT_q}{dT} = \sum_q \Omega_q \lambda_q \theta_q \tag{3.95}$$

with $\theta_q = dT_q / dT$, the marginal tax proportion paid by individual q.

For non-discriminating social weights Ω_q, a social utility of money can be calculated as a weighted average of individual marginal utilities of income, using marginal tax proportions as weights. Irrespective of which social factor λ_s we use to convert W into money, the term that multiplies Δt_q in (3.91) modified by λ_s is the *SPT* of individual q under the welfare approach.

Definition 3.5: Social price of time
The social price of time is defined as

$$SPT_q = \Omega_q \frac{\lambda_q}{\lambda_s} SVTTS_q \tag{3.96}$$

Then, even if $SVTTS_q = w_q$, the SPT_q would not be given by the wage rate within this framework. Note that for SPT_q to be equal to $SVTTS_q$, the social weight attached to individual (or group) q should be inversely related with λ_q, or directly related with income,

$$SPT_q = SVTTS_q \Rightarrow \Omega_q \frac{\lambda_q}{\lambda_s} = 1 \Rightarrow \frac{\partial W_s}{\partial U_q} = \frac{\lambda_s}{\lambda_q} \tag{3.97}$$

This reveals the highly regressive assumptions behind the acceptance of the subjective value as the social price of time: since people with higher income have lower marginal utility of income, the wealthier the person, the more important his/her time is valued by society when analyzing transport projects.

If we choose to impose $\left(\partial W_s / \partial U_q\right) = 1, \forall q$, i.e. all groups or all individuals have the same social weight, then the social price of time is

$$SPT_q = \frac{\lambda_q}{\lambda_s} SVTTS_q \qquad (3.98)$$

The *SVTTS* is usually calculated from travel choice models as seen in Chapter 2, such that it is always equal to the marginal utility of travel time $\partial V_i / \partial t_i$ divided by the marginal utility of cost, and this latter is identically equal to minus the marginal utility of income in discrete choice models. Replacing this in equation (3.98) we get the most synthetic form for the social price of time under the welfare approach with non-discriminating social weights, which is

$$SPT_q = \frac{|\partial V_i / \partial t_i|_q}{\lambda_s}. \qquad (3.99)$$

Note that using *SPT* does not mean imposing a single value of time for the whole population, as it depends on the *perception* of travel time and not on its private *value*, which can differ across groups. Therefore, whether a single or several social values of time should be used becomes essentially an empirical matter, which is quite an unbiased approach.

This result shows how relevant are the elements that determine the marginal utility of travel time as discussed in Chapter 2, i.e. the perception of goods, leisure, work and travel time as arguments in direct utility. If people's own valuation of their time is used to determine what projects society should prioritize, tax money will go proportionally more to high income groups. If a social framework is used instead, the subjective value of time should never be used to evaluate social projects.

In summary, behind the derivation of a social price of time lies a correction of consumer's surplus in order to turn it into a social value *given a viewpoint of how individual welfares should be aggregated to determine society's welfare.* And this is something that can be applied to any qualitative change that affects individual utility. Therefore, equation (3.99) can be extended to calculate social values of important aspects as pollution, safety, etc. (see Jara-Díaz *et al.* 2000, 2006).

3.6. Synthesis

Improving transport systems induces conditions which are perceived as more satisfactory by users; they indeed constitute a benefit. It poses the problem of turning the subjective perception of that improvement into monetary units, for proper comparison with costs. In this chapter, the operational approaches to solve this problem have been presented, emphasizing their economic foundations in an effort to provide an integrating view of them.

Individuals' perceptions are observed through transport demand, which relates travel needs to the characteristics of transport systems. It has been shown that the information behind demand is sufficient to account for all benefits accruing to the different agents in those markets which are affected by changes in transport conditions. The relation between both market and compensated demands and the valuation of consumers' benefits has been strictly established; however, the most widely used tool to assess users' benefits, the rule-of-a-half, does not use the analytical form of demand, requiring only the initial and final states. The intuitively motivated rule-of-a-half is shown to be, even under its most general expression, an approximation to the least rigorous but most popular form of welfare measure: the Marshallian consumers' surplus. A departure from RH leads to more rigorous forms of users' benefits, which consider demand models explicitly in their derivation, thus including the information provided by the different elements involved in transport demand. Furthermore, explicit derivation of such rigorous welfare measures allows a better interpretation of benefits in terms of demand parameters and their underlying meaning. From this viewpoint, benefit measures have been obtained for the so-called direct demand models, the family of entropy models, and the family of discrete choice models.

By showing that transport demand derives from the economic environment, it has been proved that user's benefits do capture the impact of transport improvements in those competitive markets that generate transport demand. When competition does not prevail in production, this equivalence weakens with monopoly power.

There is one aspect which cannot be regarded as further sophistication of available approaches, but as a systematically omitted element: the role of income. The usual excuse to relegate income to a secondary place has been the presumably low relevance of transport in individuals' budgets; the fact is the observed structure of household expenditure in wide socio-economic groups in developing nations does not support such an assumption. As seen here, income elasticity does play a role in the analysis of welfare changes within the Hicksian framework, particularly in the quality of proposed approximations of market demands as compensated ones. We have derived an approximation of the Compensating Variation (CV) in terms of market demands, where careful use of the Slutsky equation plays an important part. Viewed in this way, CV has been interpreted as a sum of the traditional Marshallian welfare measure plus an income-induced welfare impact (IWI), which represents the contribution of the income effect to the valuation of users' benefits.

Finally, aggregation of individuals' benefits for project evaluation will always include explicit or implicit judgments, since the (money equivalent of) utility of several individuals or groups have to be added. How important is the welfare of one individual relative to another is an area that falls in the boundary of ideology and politics. Here we have shown that the simple addition of the ΔMCS hides a preference for high income groups. A proper social price calculation for travel time savings has been presented, which can be extended to other qualitative aspects of travel.

4. Optimal Transport Pricing

4.1. Introduction

The fare of a transport service influences its number of users. Or in a more general case, if there is a set of transport modes we can see as alternatives, then all modes prices will play a role determining the number of users each mode will receive. Although prices could be seen only as a result of market equilibrium, fares do play a role in users' behavior - something we have seen in Chapter 2- and therefore we may ask what types of outcomes arise from different pricing strategies.

On the other hand, if prices are not seen as a by-product of market equilibrium, but as a tool to influence behavior from a regulatory perspective or simply as a control variable able to generate an outcome deemed desirable -which may be the case of public companies for example- then the question about optimal pricing becomes even more interesting. In such scenario it is worth asking how different the resulting social benefit is compared to the market case, or if the resulting fares are even able to cover firm's costs. Is the predefined objective financially viable? What is the role of demand's elasticity to price? What are the consequences in terms of other key variables such as patronage?

The fact that people normally do have alternative transport modes to choose from, clearly adds more complexity to this whole pricing issue, yet allows new relevant questions: if we can set the fare of only one mode, can that decision have an impact on the entire market such that we could correct the problems of economic inefficiency generated by other modes?

This chapter covers these topics, starting the analysis with the simple view of transport as a single-product industry, to examine then the more realistic multi-product case, for which applications are presented using the popular Logit model. The single-product case is nevertheless useful to discuss optimal pricing differences between private and public transport. In this Chapter the role of costs, demand and users' benefits emerge in an integrated fashion.

4.2. Optimal pricing in the single output case

Changes in prices lead to demand variations, which in turn have an impact on transport costs. Inversely put, costs depend on demand level, and demand depends on prices. In time, changes in these three variables imply changes on other relevant figures, namely, consumer benefits, patronage, and transport firms' revenues and profits. If we denote prices by P, demand by $Y(P)$ and transport costs by $C(Y)$, we can summarize these basic ideas as in Figure 4.1, where subscripts refer to different modes.

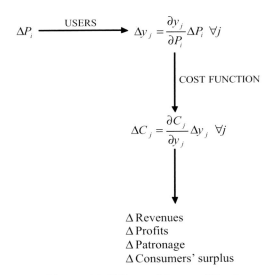

Figure 4.1. *Effects of fare modifications.*

The concept of an "optimal price" can only be developed once we define what is desirable and that is normally a policy decision, either of private or public origin. In what follows, four possible criteria for defining "desirable" will be considered –namely, maximization of users' benefits, firms' profits, social benefits and patronage- and their associated optimal prices will be derived.

a)   Maximize users' benefits (consumers' viewpoint)

The objective function is to maximize the Marshallian Consumers' Surplus (*MCS*), as defined in the previous chapter. A simple graphical analysis shows that the maximum of this function is reached when $P=0$, that is, when $Y=Y^I$ in Figure 4.2.

$$\text{Max } MCS \Rightarrow P = P^1 = 0$$
$$Y = Y^1 = Y(0)$$

(4.1)

b)   Maximize profit (private operator's viewpoint)

The profit p of a private operator is the total revenue R, minus the total cost C, i.e.

$$\pi = R - C = P(Y)Y - C(Y)$$

(4.2)

$$\text{Max } \pi \Rightarrow \frac{d\pi}{dY} = 0 \qquad (4.3)$$

$$\Leftrightarrow \quad \frac{d(P(Y)Y)}{dY} - \frac{dC(Y)}{dY} = 0 \qquad (4.4)$$

$$\Leftrightarrow \quad r(Y) - m(Y) = 0 \qquad (4.5)$$

where $r(Y) = \dfrac{d(P(Y)Y)}{dY} = P + Y\dfrac{dP}{dY}$ is the marginal revenue and $m(Y) = \dfrac{dC(Y)}{dY}$ is the marginal cost. Replacing these in equation (4.5) one gets

$$\frac{(P-m)}{P} = \frac{-1}{\dfrac{dY}{dP}\dfrac{P}{Y}} = \frac{1}{|\eta|} \qquad (4.6)$$

where η is the price elasticity of demand. This is represented by point (Y^2, P^2) in Figure 4.2.

c)   Maximize social benefits (economic efficiency viewpoint)

This case consists of maximizing the total benefit of the system, including users and operators; i.e. maximizing social benefits.

$$SB = \pi + \Delta MCS = P(Y) - C(Y) + \Delta MCS \qquad (4.7)$$

$$\text{Max } SB = \pi + \Delta MCS \Rightarrow \frac{d(\pi + \Delta MCS)}{dY} = 0 \qquad (4.8)$$

$$\Leftrightarrow P(Y) + Y\frac{dP}{dY} - m(Y) - Y\frac{dP}{dY} = 0 \qquad (4.9)$$

$$\Leftrightarrow P(Y^3) = m(Y^3) \qquad (4.10)$$

Not surprisingly, the optimal fare is $P^3 = P(Y^3) = m(Y^3)$, meaning the optimal pricing should match marginal cost, which is a rather known result when seeking economic efficiency. The solution can be graphically represented by point (P^3, Y^3) in Figure 4.2. Note $P^3 < P^2$ and $Y^3 > Y^2$.

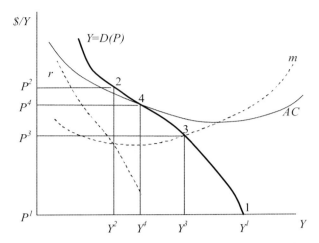

Figure 4.2. *Optimal prices for different objectives in the single output case*

This optimal social fare (equal to marginal cost) may or may not cover production costs. This is a central point for transport firms, as a subsidy could be necessary for financial viability. Clearly, to cover costs we need price to be at least equal to the average cost AC (we charge each person what moving an average person costs), so if price is set equal to marginal cost as derived above, the only question will be if average costs are above or below marginal costs, which in time means asking about the firm's degree of scale economies. Analytically, the condition $\pi \geq 0$ translates into:

$$P = m \geq AC \Leftrightarrow \frac{AC}{m} \leq 1 \Leftrightarrow S \leq 1 \tag{4.11}$$

where S is the degree of scale economies according to equation (1.23). In other words, if the firm operates in the decreasing returns to scale range, the social optimum is financially viable. What if there are increasing returns to scale, thus making the system unable to finance itself, but yet the service is deemed necessary? Two alternatives: a subsidy or, if not feasible, a price such that costs are covered while keeping welfare as high as possible. The latter corresponds to the solution of

$$\text{Max } SB = (\pi + MCS)$$
$$\text{subject to } \pi \geq 0 \tag{4.12}$$

The solution, known as *second best* because economic efficiency is not reached, is quite simple in the single output case. As suggested by equation (4.11), the solution is $P = AC$, which is represented by point (Y^4, P^4) in Figure 4.2.

d)   Maximize patronage

This is equivalent to case a); as costs are not covered and demand decrease with price monotonically, maximizing patronage subject to a budget constraint yields price equal to average cost.

It should be recalled that the social benefit, which is the sum of users' benefits and firms' profits, also corresponds to the total willingness to pay by users (*WP*) minus the total cost. This, which will be used in the next section, is graphically shown in Figure 4.3.

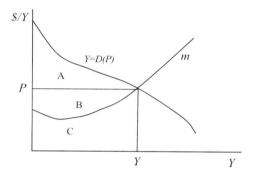

A=Consumer's surplus; B=Firms' profits; C=Production Costs;
A+B+C=Willingness to pay
Figure 4.3. *Social benefits as willingness to pay minus production costs, or as consumer surplus plus firms' profits*

4.3. Extension to transport systems

4.3.1. A general optimal price

The key issue when translating the general results from the previous section to the transport industry is realizing that firms do not provide *all* economic resources to produce the final good (transport) because passengers have to put in their time. **Unlike other industries, accounting for all economic resources (total cost) in order to find an optimal pricing scheme leads to acknowledging that a rather important and valuable resource, individuals' time, is provided by consumers themselves and not by firms.**

That said one may nevertheless suspect that an optimal fare still would depend only on firms' costs like in any other market, because even though consumers are providing their precious time as a "production input", they are simultaneously and instantly "paying" for it as their time is consumed along the journey. Although there is some truth in this thought, we shall see it is not entirely correct.

To start our analysis, total costs will be divided in two groups: those provided by the operators, as vehicles, fuel, terminals or labor, and those provided by the users, namely their time, usually divided into waiting, access and in-vehicle time. Total cost (C_T) can be written as

$$C_T = C_{op} + C_U \tag{4.13}$$

where C_{op} and C_U are the operators' and users' total costs, respectively. C_U is of course users' total time multiplied by the value of time (or the sum of access, waiting and in-vehicle times multiplied by their respective time valuations), and consequently the cost of each user is C_U/Y, where Y is the demand level (number of users). In other words, a user's cost is the users' average cost, AC_U.

As for demand Y, it obviously depends on AC_U, but it is also sensitive to the fare P that users are required to pay in money. Then, we can use the concept of generalized cost introduced in the previous chapter, defining

$$GC = P + AC_U \tag{4.14}$$

and seeing Y as a function of GC.

We will concentrate our analysis in *social* optimal pricing, i.e. maximizing economic efficiency, since that is the world's currently preferred view when examining markets, but it should be clear the analysis could also be made with other optimal criteria with no difficulties. Maximizing social benefits becomes, then:

$$\text{Max } SB = \pi + \Delta MCS = WP - C = \int_0^Y GC(u)\,du - \left[C_{op}(Y) + C_U(Y) \right] \tag{4.15}$$

where GC in the integral is the inverse demand function. The first order condition for (4.15) is

$$\frac{\partial SB}{\partial Y} = GC(Y^*) - m_{op}(Y^*) - m_U(Y^*) = 0 \tag{4.16}$$

where m_{op} and m_U are the operators' and users' marginal costs, respectively. Using (4.14) and given that the total marginal cost (m_T) is the sum of m_{op} and m_U, the optimal fare is

$$P^* = m_T(Y^*) - AC_U(Y^*) \tag{4.17}$$

This equation states that the user has to pay (in money) the difference between total marginal cost and users' average cost. It is important to realize this difference is reflecting the fact that the user is already "paying" for part of the costs -the time he or she spends traveling- and that is why the actual required payment only accounts for all other costs the journey implies.

Note now that by writing users' marginal cost as

$$m_U = \frac{d(Y \cdot AC_U)}{dY} = AC_U + Y\frac{dAC_U}{dY} \qquad (4.18)$$

then the total marginal cost can be written as

$$m_T = m_{op} + AC_U + Y\frac{dAC_U}{dY} \qquad (4.19)$$

and replacing in (4.17) we get an alternative expression for the optimal fare (Jansson, 1979):

$$P^* = m_{op}\Big|_{Y^*} + Y^* \frac{dAC_U}{dY}\Big|_{Y^*} \qquad (4.20)$$

The value and the concept is obviously the same as in (4.17), but this expression is more revealing. It says the user has to pay for the increase his or her trip is causing to the transport operator's cost, *plus* the increase that trip is causing to users' average cost, multiplied by the demand level. The former was expected; the latter is the interesting one.

Basically, **the second term in (4.20) is saying a user has to pay for the time consumption variation he or she is inducing *on everybody else*.** If this trip by this new user makes everybody else consume more time, which is the case when the derivative is positive, then for economic efficiency a payment -additional to operator's marginal cost- is required. Conversely, if the new trip makes everyone else consume less time traveling, the new user should be "rewarded" paying less than operator's marginal cost.

We are here evidently in front of a negative or positive externality depending on the effect of new users over the remaining users. And it is the presence of this externality that explains why our intuition was only partially correct above when we started: time as an economic resource, or even better, as a "production input" in this industry, provided not by firms but by consumer themselves, does make a difference because even though each user is simultaneously and instantly providing and consuming its own time in this process, at the same time is demanding an increase or decrease of other economic resources, namely, other individuals' time. Unless that change in demanded resources is paid or rewarded for, the market will not be socially efficient.

4.3.2. Particular case 1: Private transport

In the private transport case, the user and the operator are the same person, so the first term in expression (4.20), the operators' marginal cost, simply represents the expenses −fuel, lubricants and spare parts basically- a driver has to face to get his/her vehicle running, plus the cost of the associated infrastructure. This term is of course positive and can be safely assumed to be equal to the average operator's cost.

As for the second term, since it is part of our common experience, it is probably unnecessary to exhibit the vast body of evidence showing that the increase of new users in the case of the private transport market implies an increase of users' average cost in the presence of congestion. New car drivers do make everyone else consume more time traveling, so the derivative in expression (4.20) is positive, meaning the externality is negative, and therefore users should pay for causing it.

Each new car driver experiences congestion, including the extra delay he or she is generating, but this driver does not perceive the additional time consumption the rest of car drivers experience as a result of this new vehicle entering the system. **The new driver perceives the average cost AC_U but not (the higher) social marginal cost.**

A graphical view of this situation is shown in Figure 4.4, where the role of implementing a charge P^* equal to (4.20) or (4.17), a "congestion charge", can also be seen: the increase of the mode's cost (the mode's generalized cost) due to this charge provokes $Y^1 - Y^2$ number of users decide to stop traveling by car to avoid the payment (perhaps shifting to public transport), and that improves speeds reducing travel times. By construction the new total number of users, Y^2, matches the optimal number of drivers this market (road) should have for economic efficiency purposes. Congestion charging is, clearly, *a tool to induce a specific behavior* for the sake of efficiency / social benefits.

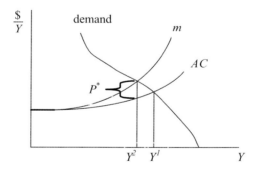

Figure 4.4. *Optimal pricing in the private transport market*

4.3.3. Particular case 2: Public transport

It is less obvious what happens with expression (4.20) in the case of (scheduled) public transport. We do have now two different agents as in our general analysis, operators and users. What is the effect of an extra user?

Let us examine separately the components of total cost, C_{op} and C_U, and their behavior as demand grows, starting by the former. Operators incur in operational and capital costs.

Operational costs include energy, crew, maintenance and administration, and capital costs involve infrastructure and rolling stock. How do they look like in total? Engineering cost studies have found that **average operator costs decrease with demand** (Meyer *et al.*, 1965; Boyd *et al.*, 1978; Allport, 1981) meaning there are economies of scale. That should be easy to see: fixed infrastructure such as terminals, stations, railways, power lines, etc, need not to grow proportionally to demand. Vehicles as well, although in lesser degree, do not need either to grow at the same pace as demand does.

Let us turn now our attention to C_U (users' time) and how it changes with growing demand. We should analyze separately its three different parts; access, waiting and in-vehicle time:

- In-vehicle time: the quickest response from operators to increasing demand is improving frequency, which is the simplest measure to take (within certain limits). But higher frequencies lead to more vehicle interactions (congestion), thus increasing in-vehicle time. Not only that, additional passengers also make boarding and alighting time grow, which increases in-vehicle time as well.

- Waiting time: clearly, if demand grows and operators respond increasing frequency, waiting times diminish.

- Access time: if routes can be adapted, increasing demand will lead to reduced access times, as operators will be able to expand routes to reach these new customers.

In summary, when demand increases, users' in-vehicle time grows due to both vehicle congestion and passengers boarding/alighting; waiting time always diminishes; and access time decreases only if routes can be adapted. A general conclusion for C_U may seem elusive, and it may even seem that the answer can change from one public transport mode to another, since route adaptation feasibility, for example, is clearly quite different with buses or trains. But this qualitative analysis actually yields a common scheme for the relation between users' cost and demand. On one hand, bus-like modes have higher probability of congestion, but at the same time they are the most flexible regarding routes expansion. On the other hand, the rigid rail-based modes have little (tram) or no (underground) congestion likelihood, while route adaptation involves serious effort. So, with bus-like modes a demand growth makes in-vehicle and access times vary with opposite signs, while with rail modes both changes are low or negligible. Therefore, it is the waiting time that prevails, and that means **a decreasing average users' cost function** (AC_U) **with demand in all cases**. That is, $\partial AC_U/\partial Y$ is negative and reflects the positive externality an extra user generates: **a new passenger pushes the system to increase frequency and/or coverage, thus benefiting all other users.**

The conclusion is that the sum of the operators' and users' costs yields a total cost that grows less than proportional with demand, as found by Boyd *et al.* (1978) and Allport (1981) in their engineering cost studies. This means total average cost decreases with demand, which implies the public transport case presents scale economies, as opposed to the private transport case, and consequently public transport passengers are not required to pay for externalities as car drivers are.

Now, since $\partial AC_U/\partial Y$ is negative, from expression (4.20) we see the optimal public transport fare must be lower than operators' marginal cost. Operators' costs are clearly not covered under this situation, which can be seen subtracting operators' average cost from both sides of (4.17):

$$P^* - AC_{op}(Y^*) = m_T(Y^*) - AC_T(Y^*) \tag{4.21}$$

As AC_T is larger than m_T, operators' average cost is larger than P^*. Expenses are not covered and a subsidy per passenger s^*, equal to the difference between AC_{op} and P^* is necessary. Expression (4.21) indicates this optimal subsidy is equal to the difference between AC_T and m_T as well, which is shown in Figure 4.5.

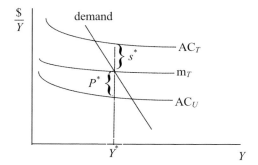

Figure 4.5. *Optimal fare and subsidy in public transport.*

So, summarizing private and public transport cases, if economic efficiency is desired, car drivers must be charged to account for the increased times they impose on other car drivers, while scheduled public transport fares should be lower than operators' marginal cost, accompanied by a subsidy to the firms to make them financially viable. However, it should be clear the analysis made here has assumed sharply separated markets between private vehicles and public transport. Although that can be true given a physically divided network (as a subway is separated from cars' roadways, for example), we know in most cases private and public transport do share infrastructure -roads- and therefore both solutions (optimal prices) are related.

The next section deals with the issue of competing modes either efficiently or inefficiently priced, but nevertheless it is important to state here two things about modes that share infrastructure that should be evident from our recent conclusions:

- The possible congestion caused by public transport vehicles to users of other modes is subject to a congestion charge as any other vehicle, and should be included in the calculation of the optimal fare.

- The negative externality cars produce increases when sharing the road with public transport vehicles, as each new driver imposes delays on far more people. Consequently, the magnitude of the congestion charge increases as well.

4.4. Optimal fares with multiple outputs

4.4.1. General solutions

As transport firms produce several outputs, the multiple output case is much more interesting and realistic in the transport industry. In order to simplify the analytical treatment, let us study the n output case with independent demands and a linear cost function, which is represented by

$$y_i = D_i(P_i) \tag{4.22}$$

$$C(y_1, y_2, ..., y_n) = F + \sum_{i=1}^{n} m_i y_i \tag{4.23}$$

Note that choosing m_i to name the parameter multiplying output y_i in the cost function is not casual; m_i is obviously the marginal cost with respect to y_i so this way we can keep our notation consistent. Deriving optimal prices for different optimality criteria now follows.

a)   Maximize users' benefit

This case has a trivial solution, i.e. $P_i = 0$, $\forall i \in \{1, ..., n\}$

b)   Maximize profit

The firm's viewpoint has a solution analogous to the single output case. The objective function is

$$\pi = R - C = \sum_{j=1}^{n} P_j y_j - F - \sum_{j=1}^{n} m_j y_j \tag{4.24}$$

First order conditions (FOC) are

$$\frac{\partial \pi}{\partial P_i} = y_i + P_i \frac{dy_i}{dP_i} - m_i \frac{dy_i}{dP_i} = 0 \tag{4.25}$$

$$\Leftrightarrow \frac{(P_i - m_i)}{P_i} = \frac{-1}{\dfrac{dy_i}{dP_i} \dfrac{P_i}{y_i}} = \frac{1}{|\eta_i|} \tag{4.26}$$

c)   Maximize social benefits

Just as in the single output case, the solution extends to $P_i = m_i$ $\forall i \in \{1, ..., n\}$. However, revenue and profit are, respectively,

$$R = \sum_{i=1}^{n} P_i y_i = \sum_{i=1}^{n} m_i y_i \qquad (4.27)$$

$$\pi = R - C = -F \qquad (4.28)$$

Therefore, costs are not covered. The problem can be restated by imposing a budget constraint as follows

$$\text{Max } SB = \pi + \Delta MCS = WP - C = \sum_{j=1}^{n} \int_0^{y_j} P_j dy_j - F - \sum_{j=1}^{n} m_j y_j \qquad (4.29)$$

$$\text{Subject to } \sum_{j=1}^{n} P_j y_j \geq F + \sum_{j=1}^{n} m_j y_j \qquad (4.30)$$

The Lagrange function is

$$L = \sum_{j=1}^{n} \int_0^{y_j} P_j dy_j - F - \sum_{j=1}^{n} m_j y_j + \lambda \left(\sum_{j=1}^{n} P_j y_j - F - \sum_{j=1}^{n} m_j y_j \right) \qquad (4.31)$$

where λ is the Lagrange multiplier associated to the budget restriction. Then, FOC are

$$\frac{\partial L}{\partial P_i} = P_i \frac{\partial y_i}{\partial P_i} - m_i \frac{\partial y_i}{\partial P_i} + \lambda \left(y_i + P_i \frac{\partial y_i}{\partial P_i} - m_i \frac{\partial y_i}{\partial P_i} \right) = 0 \qquad (4.32)$$

$$(m_i - P_i) \frac{\partial y_i}{\partial P_i} (1 + \lambda) = \lambda y_i \qquad (4.33)$$

and from this one gets

$$\frac{(P_i - m_i)}{P_i} = \frac{\lambda}{1 + \lambda} \frac{1}{|\eta_i|} \qquad \forall i \in \{1,...,n\} \qquad (4.34)$$

Equation (4.34) is known as **Ramsey's rule** or **Inverse Elasticity Rule** (IER). Note that if the multiplier λ is nil, then $P_i = m_i$, which is an obvious result because $\lambda = 0$ means the budget constraint is inactive, that is, costs are covered when prices equal marginal costs. As in the single output case, there will be a non-zero λ when increasing scale economies are present, and it will equal zero otherwise, because increasing returns imply costs larger than revenue.

d) Maximize patronage

The solution of the unrestricted problem is, trivially, $P_i=0 \ \forall i \in \{1,...,n\}$. For the system to be financially viable, a constraint has to be imposed, which leads to formalizing the problem as follows:

$$\text{Max} \sum_{j=1}^{n} y_j \tag{4.35}$$

$$\text{subject to } \pi \geq 0 \tag{4.36}$$

The Lagrange function is

$$L = \sum_{j=1}^{n} y_j + \lambda \left(\sum_{j=1}^{n} P_j y_j - F - \sum_{j=1}^{n} m_j y_j \right) \tag{4.37}$$

where λ is again the Lagrange multiplier associated to costs coverage. Then FOC with respect to P_i are

$$\frac{\partial L}{\partial P_i} = \frac{\partial y_i}{\partial P_i} + \lambda \left(y_i + P_i \frac{\partial y_i}{\partial P_i} - m_i \frac{\partial y_i}{\partial P_i} \right) = 0 \tag{4.38}$$

$$\frac{\partial y_i}{\partial P_i} \left[\lambda(m_i - P_i) - 1 \right] = \lambda y_i \tag{4.39}$$

And we get

$$\frac{(P_i - m_i)}{P_i} = \frac{1}{|\eta_i|} - \frac{1}{\lambda P_i} \tag{4.40}$$

e) Maximize social benefits in a market with competing modes, covering costs

This is an interesting case. What if there are several modes competing for the passengers in a single O-D pair, we are interested in maximizing social benefits, but we control the fare of only one mode? Let k be a mode which competes with other $n-1$ modes, each facing a cost function $C_j(y_j)$ and each having a fare P_j. The problem formulation, where our only control variable is mode k's fare, P_k, is:

$$\underset{P_k}{\text{Max}} \ -\sum_{j} \int_{P_j^0}^{P_j} y_j \, dP_j + \sum_{j} P_j y_j - \sum_{j} C_j(y_j) \tag{4.41}$$

$$\text{subject to } P_k y_k \geq C_k(y_k) \tag{4.42}$$

The Lagrange function is

$$L = -\sum_j \int_{P_j^0}^{P_j} y_j dP_j + \sum_j P_j y_j - \sum_j C_j(y_j) + \lambda(P_k y_k - C_k(y_k)) \tag{4.43}$$

where λ is the Lagrange multiplier associated to (4.42). Then, the FOC with respect to P_k is

$$\frac{\partial L}{\partial P_k} = \sum_j P_j \frac{\partial y_j}{\partial P_k} - \sum_j \frac{\partial C_j}{\partial y_j}\frac{\partial y_j}{\partial P_k} + \lambda\left(P_k \frac{\partial y_k}{\partial P_k} + y_k - \frac{\partial C_k}{\partial y_k}\frac{\partial y_k}{\partial P_k}\right) = 0 \tag{4.44}$$

After some algebraic work we get

$$\frac{(P_k - m_k)}{P_k} = \frac{\lambda}{1+\lambda}\frac{1}{|\eta_k|} + \frac{1}{y_k(1+\lambda)|\eta_k|}\sum_{j\neq k}(P_j - m_j)\frac{\partial y_j}{\partial P_k} \tag{4.45}$$

Two comments are worth making about this expression. First, if all other modes (other than k) have fares equal to their marginal costs, then (4.45) becomes Ramsey's rule, meaning mode k's fare can be set as if there were no other modes intervening. That is interesting, yet not surprising, because the result reflects the fact that the rest of the modes in the market behave competitively: total social benefits will be as high as mode k's financial constraint allows it. On the other hand, under the unfortunate case when all P_j are greater than the respective m_j, that is, when all the remaining modes are using fares larger (smaller) than socially efficient, then (4.45) leads to a value larger (smaller) than Ramsey's value because all price derivatives are positive for the competing modes. And this is very interesting because what mode k's fare will be doing is attempting to *correct* the market's efficiency problem. In general, expression (4.45) can be understood as a Ramsey rule plus a correcting term that reflects the efficiency situation of the rest of the market.

It is also worth mentioning that when the financial constraint is either inactive or ignored, i.e. when $\lambda = 0$, equation (4.45) collapses to the simpler expression (4.46). The comment in the previous paragraph remains valid but with reference to marginal cost pricing rather than Ramsey's.

$$\frac{(P_k - m_k)}{P_k} = \frac{1}{y_k|\eta_k|}\sum_{j\neq k}(P_j - m_j)\frac{\partial y_j}{\partial P_k} \tag{4.46}$$

4.4.2. Applications using the Logit model

Consider n modes competing in several O-D pairs, with a total demand of N_i users on each. Let $Y_k = \{y_{ki}\}$ be the flow vector for mode k, and S_{ki} be mode k's share in pair i. Cost functions are represented by $C_k(Y_k)$ and the decision variable under control by the transport operator is the vector of fares $P_k = \{P_{ki}\}$. It will be assumed that $(\partial y_{ki}/\partial P_{kj}) = 0 \ \forall i \neq j$, i.e. a fare variation in any pair j does not influence the demand in pair i.

We will use the well known Logit model to describe demand in each market, that is,

$$S_{ki} = \frac{\exp(V_{ki})}{\sum_{l=1}^{n} \exp(V_{li})} \tag{4.47}$$

And a linear specification for the indirect utility function will be considered:

$$V_{li} = \alpha_{li} + \sum_{j} \sigma_{ji} q_{lji} + \beta_i P_{li} \tag{4.48}$$

where a_{li}, s_{ji} and β_i are constants, and q_{lji} are qualities of mode k in pair i, such as (-)travel or (-) waiting time.

Given the chosen model flow vectors are $y_{ki} = N_i S_{ki}$ and the following expressions hold.

$$\frac{\partial y_{ki}}{\partial P_{km}} = 0 \ \forall i \neq m \tag{4.49}$$

$$\frac{\partial y_{ki}}{\partial P_{ki}} = N_i \beta_i S_{ki} (1 - S_{ki}) \tag{4.50}$$

$$\frac{\partial y_{li}}{\partial P_{ki}} = -N_i \beta_i S_{li} S_{ki} \tag{4.51}$$

$$\eta_{ki} = \beta_i P_{ki} (1 - S_{ki}) \tag{4.52}$$

These properties of the the Logit formulation will be used next to apply various pricing results developed earlier.

a)   Max Profit

Our general result (4.26) becomes now

$$P_{ki} = m_{ki} + \frac{1}{|\beta_i|(1 - S_{ki})} \tag{4.53}$$

As S_{ki} is a function of P_{ki}, this is a fixed-point equation for the optimal fare, to be computed iteratively. Note each component of Y_k generates an independent problem. Consider also that equation (4.53) is equivalent to make marginal revenue match marginal cost, which solution in the single product case is point 2 shown in Figure 4.2. The importance of β_i (which reflects demand sensitivity to price) is clear in (4.53); the more reactive the population to fares, the closest it should be to marginal costs in order to maximize profits. Typical values of β_i, however, yield fares much higher than the marginal cost.

b)   Max social benefits (unconstrained)

Applying (4.46) and using the appropriate analytical properties exposed above, P_{ki} is given by

$$P_{ki} = m_{ki} + \sum_{l \neq k}(P_{li} - m_{li})\frac{S_{li}}{1 - S_{ki}} \tag{4.54}$$

Our result this time needs not to be computed iteratively as in the previous case because the right hand term does not depend on P_{ki} . That can be seen noting that

$$1 - S_{ki} = \sum_{l \neq k} S_{li} \tag{4.55}$$

and therefore,

$$\frac{S_{li}}{1 - S_{ki}} = \frac{S_{li}}{\sum\limits_{r \neq k} S_{ri}} = \frac{\exp(V_{li})}{\sum\limits_{r \neq k} \exp(V_{ri})} \tag{4.56}$$

which is an expression not dependent on P_{ki}.

Equation (4.54) shows that, in general, the social optimal fare differs from marginal cost by an amount given by the weighted sum of differences between other modes' prices and marginal costs. Weights are all positive and add up to 1, so this is more a combination of those differences, with each element proportionally important to a monotonic transformation of its market participation.

Note also that under congested conditions, if automobiles are one of the competing modes and they are not subject to a congestion charge, then its associated P_{li}-m_{li} will be negative because P_{li} will be equal to car drivers' average cost. In consequence, the presence of cars as an alternative will push optimal fares of all other modes downwards. In other words, setting one mode's price at marginal cost is good only if all other alternatives are also priced as such.

c)   Max social benefits covering costs (*second best*)

As there are competing modes and cost coverage is intended, the solution comes from equation (4.45), which for our Logit model takes the form

$$P_{ki} = m_{ki} + \frac{1}{(1 + \lambda)(1 - S_{ki})}\left[\frac{\lambda}{|\beta_i|} + \sum_{l \neq k}(P_{li} - m_{li})S_{li}\right] \tag{4.57}$$

If $\lambda = 0$, i.e. costs are covered, (4.57) collapses into our previous result, (4.54). If $\lambda > 0$, the budget constraint provides the extra equation to solve the system in prices and λ . In general, optimal price in markets where users exhibit a high sensitivity to fares ($|\beta_i|$) will be closer to marginal cost.

On the other hand, if the set of available modes presents prices equal to marginal costs, then equation (4.57) would turn into

$$P_{ki} = m_{ki} + \frac{\theta}{|\beta_i|(1 - S_{ki})} \qquad (4.58)$$

where $\theta = \lambda/(1 + \lambda)$. This last equation is the aforementioned inverse elasticity rule, which indicates that the proportion in which prices deviate from marginal costs should follow the inverse of its price elasticity of demand. As $\lambda \geq 0$, θ lies between 0 and 1, i.e. optimal prices lie between the marginal cost and the profit maximizing fare.

d) Maximize patronage covering costs

The solution we found for the general case, equation (4.40), becomes in this case

$$P_{ki} = m_{ki} - \frac{1}{\lambda} + \frac{1}{|\beta_i|(1 - S_{ki})} \qquad (4.59)$$

or

$$P_{ki} = 0 \ \ if \ \ m_{ki} - \frac{1}{\lambda} + \frac{1}{|\beta_i|(1 - S_{ki})} < 0 \qquad (4.60)$$

When the covering costs condition is active, the Lagrange multiplier λ is positive and, as expected, optimal fares are lower than the ones found for the max profit case. The resulting fare structure tends to discriminate in favor of more fare-sensitive users and those who have a lower marginal cost. In practice, the solutions from equations (4.59) and (4.60) can generate very large disparities among users. Imposing a minimum fare equal to marginal cost would diminish this effect while imposing a reasonable floor equal to the value of the extra resources needed to carry an extra passenger.

4.4.3. Role of individuals' sensitivity to price and quality

It can be seen that only in the unconstrained max social benefit case the solution does not depend on people's sensitivity to price, β. This variable plays a clear role in the remaining scenarios, so for example in the max profit case a lower sensitivity to price allows increasing the fare to levels much higher than marginal cost because demand decreases less than proportionally. A warning is needed here regarding the value of $|\beta|$ interacting with the mode shares in practice, as in estimated models the value of $|\beta|(1 - S)$ could be very small for public transport modes in O-D pairs where users are either captive or have expensive alternatives only, usually low income areas.

But more generally, what is the role of the sensitivity to service level? In order to answer this question, equation (4.53) will be used to assess the effect of travel time over the maximum profit fares. Omitting the market index, we can define

$$g(P_k, t_k) = P_k - m_k - \frac{1}{|\beta|[1 - S(P_k, t_k)]}$$ (4.61)

where t_k is the travel time, whose influence over P_k can be assessed from the implicit function $g(P_k, t_k)$. It is easy to show that

$$\frac{dP_k}{dt_k} = -\frac{\partial g/\partial t_k}{\partial g/\partial P_k} = -\frac{\sigma}{\beta} S_k < 0$$ (4.62)

where $\sigma < 0$ is the coefficient of travel time in the demand model. Then, lower travel time (better service level) implies a higher profit maximizing price, as expected. Even more, this effect grows with the subjective value of time, σ/β. A similar conclusion is found in the max patronage case given by equation (4.59). On the other hand, as can be seen from equation (4.57), the best social fare of mode k does not depend on its own service level unless the cost constraint is active. In others words, those markets where users perceive time as more valuable allow higher fares when discrimination is possible.

4.5. Synthesis and discussion

It has been shown that optimal pricing in transport systems requires different levels of information, depending on the objective pursued and constraints considered. The *first best* fare only needs good estimations of marginal costs associated to the different services provided. Note that the multiproduct approach depicted in Chapter 1 is of great help here.

The simplest case incorporating demand information besides costs is profit maximization, as the fare for each transport service (market) can be calculated independently from equation (4.53), provided demands for different services are not interrelated and marginal costs associated to a flow y_i do not depend on others flows. In this case, knowing the coefficients of utility in a Logit model allows the calculation of optimal price using equation (4.53), which is a numerically simple fixed-point problem.

On the other extreme, setting the fare for the max social benefit case needs more information, because calculation requires knowing, potentially, prices, marginal costs and demands for all the markets and modes (equation (4.54)). The case is even more difficult if a budget constraint is imposed (equation (4.57)). Unfortunately, the interdependence of marginal costs among different O-D pairs for different modes constitutes a serious problem. Think for example about congestion where buses and cars interact, or a frequency variation in a bus line induced by changes in the flows somewhere else in the network. Yet, the particular case in which other modes are priced at marginal cost (or this condition is assumed as a simplification) can be solved numerically in a relatively simple manner. Following equation (4.58), one can note that for a given value of θ, a series of independent fixed-point equations are obtained, from which fares can be calculated and the budget constraint can be verified. This generates an obvious procedure to calculate the optimal prices, by simply changing the value of θ in the appropriate direction between 0 and 1.

In terms of information requirements, patronage maximization fares from equation (4.59) seem to be no more demanding than the max welfare case from equation (4.58), as λ could be simply added to the marginal cost. However, there are two additional difficulties: there is no upper bound for λ and the corner solution represented by equation (4.60) does introduce the need to verify more than the budget constraint.

Additionally, from the examples exposed, it can be seen that:

- Fares which maximize profit are, naturally, the largest; they can reach levels much higher than marginal cost.

- Max patronage fares covering costs tend to benefit groups who make less trips and those more sensitive to price; if both conditions are present simultaneously, the benefit for the community is substantial and the individual damage on the remaining users is lower.

- Unilaterally optimal modal fares under a policy of max social benefit depend on several factors, so it is difficult to generalize a rule. These fares receive an influence from the differences between fares and marginal costs in the other modes, which can be positive or negative.

Finally, it is important to mention that optimal fares shown in this chapter, particularly those calculated for a mode competing with others, may require a sophisticated implementation strategy, meaning the response by the competition must be taken into account. In other words, in the real world setting the fare for one mode at a given magnitude, will normally force the remaining modes to change theirs as well in an attempt to neutralize potential customers losses. If such reactions occur, the implemented optimal fare will automatically become obsolete (it will no longer be optimal), as this fare depends on the competing modes' prices. Game theory or other similar approaches may be useful in these situations because they provide a way to model agents' reactions and counter-reactions, allowing us to anticipate the expected equilibrium of the system, and therefore determining the right fare to implement to reach our goal. The key here is to see that what matters is not the magnitude of a price by itself, but its relative magnitude with respect to the remaining modes' prices. It is the price structure, at the end, which is optimal or not.

References

Allport, R.J. (1981) The costing of bus, light rail transit and metro public transport systems. *Traffic Engineering and Control* 22, 633-639.

Anas, A. (1983) Discrete choice theory, information theory and the multinomial Logit and gravity models. *Transportation Research* 17B, 13-23.

Baltagi, B.H., Griffin, J.M. and Rich, D.P. (1995) Airline Deregulation: The Cost Pieces of the Puzzle. *International Economic Review* 36(1), 245-258.

Basso, L. and S.R. Jara-Díaz (2005) Calculation of economies of spatial scope from transport cost functions with aggregate output. *Journal of Transport Economics and Policy* 39, 25-52.

Basso, L. and S.R. Jara-Díaz (2006) Are Returns to Scale with variable network size adequate for transport industry structure analysis?. *Transportation Science* 40, 259-268.

Bates, J. (1987) Measuring travel time values with a discrete choice model: a note. *The Economic Journal*, 97, 493 - 498.

Bates, J. and M. Roberts (1986) Value of time research: summary of methodology and findings. *PTRC Summer Annual Meeting.*

Baumol, W.J., J.C. Panzar and R.D. Willig (1982) *Contestable markets and the theory of industry structure*. New York: Harcourt Brace Jovanovich.

Becker, G. (1965) A theory of the allocation of time. *The Economic Journal* 75, 493 - 517.

Berechman, J. (1983) Costs, economies of scale and factor demand in bus transport. *Journal of Transport Economics and Policy* 17, 7-24.

Berechman, J. (1987) Cost structure and production technology in transit. *Regional Science and Urban Economics* 17, 519-534.

Berechman, J. and G. Giuliano (1984) Analysis of the cost structure of an urban bus transit property. *Regional Science and Urban Economics* 17, 519-534.

Boyd, J.H., N.J. Asher and E.S. Wetzler (1978) Nontechnological innovation in urban transit: a comparison of some alternative. *Journal of Urban Economics* 5, 1-20.

Braeutigam, R.R., A.F. Daughety and M.A. Turnquist (1980) The estimation of a hybrid cost function for a railroad firm. *Review of Economics and Statistics* 62, 394-403.

Brueckner, J.K. and P.T. Spiller (1994) Economies of Traffic Density in the Deregulated Airline industry. *The Journal of Law and Economics* 37(2), 379-413.

Carlton, D. (1979) Valuing market benefits and costs in related output and input markets. *American Economic Review* 69, 688-696.

Caves, D.W., L.R. Christensen and J.A. Swanson (1980) Productivity in U.S. railroads, 1951-1974. *Bell Journal of Economics* 11, 166-181.

Caves, D.W., L.R. Christensen and J.A. Swanson (1981) Productivity growth, scale economies, and capacity utilisation in U.S. railroads, 1955-74. *American Economic Review* 71, 994-1002.

Caves, D.W., L.R. Christensen, and M.W. Tretheway (1984) Economies of density versus economies of scale: why trunk and local service airline costs differ. *Rand Journal of Economics* 15, 471-489.

Caves, D.W., L.R. Christensen, M.W. Tretheway and R.J. Windle (1985) Network effects and the measurement of returns to scale and density for U.S. railroads. In A.F. Daughety, ed., *Analytical Studies in Transport Economics*, Cambridge: Cambridge University Press, 97-120.

Christensen, L.R, D.W. Jorgenson and L.J. Lau (1973) Transcendental logarithmic production frontiers. *Review of Economics and Statistics* 55, 28-45.

Creel, M and M. Farell (2001) Economies of Scale in the US Airline Industry after Deregulation: A Fourier Series Approximation. *Transportation Research E*, 37, 321-336.

Dalvi, Q. (1978) Economics theories of travel choice. In: D. Hensher and Q. Dalvi, eds., *Determinants of travel choice*. Farnborough: Saxon House.

Daughety, A.F., F.D. Nelson and W.R. Vigdor (1985) An econometric analysis of the cost and production structure of the trucking industry. In A.F. Daughety, ed., *Analytical Studies in Transport Economics*, Cambridge: Cambridge University Press, 65-95.

De Donnea, E (1971) Consumer behaviour, transport mode choice and value of time: Some microeconomic models. *Regional and Urban Economics* 1, 355-382.

DeSerpa, A. (1971) A theory of the economics of time. *The Economic Journal* 81, 828 - 846.

Diamond, P. and D. McFadden (1974) Some uses of the expenditure function in public finance. *Journal of Public Economics* 3, 3 -22.

Evans, A. (1972) On the theory of the valuation and allocation of time. *Scottish Journal of Political Economy*, 1-17.

Filippini, M. and R. Maggi (1992) The cost structure of the Swiss private railways, *International Journal of Transport Economics* 19, 307-327.

Formby, J.P., P.D. Thistle and J.P. Keeler (1990) Costs under regulation and deregulation: the case of US passenger airlines *Economic Record*, 66, 308-321.

Friedlaender, A.F. and S.S. Bruce (1985) Augmentation effects and technical change in the regulated trucking industry, 1974-1979. In A.F. Daughety, ed., *Analytical Studies in Transport Economics*, Cambridge: Cambridge University Press, 29-63.

Gagné, R. (1990) On the relevant elasticity estimates for cost structure analyses of the trucking industry, *Review of Economics and Statistics* 72, 160-164.

Gálvez, T. (1978) *Análisis de operaciones en Sistemas de Transporte* (Operations analysis in transport systems), Publication ST-INV/04/78, Santiago de Chile: Universidad de Chile, Departamento de Obras Civiles.

Gálvez, T. and S.R. Jara-Díaz (1998) On the social valuation of travel time savings. *International Journal of Transport Economics* 25(2), 205-219.

Gillen, D., Oum, T.H. and Threteway, M. (1985) *Airline Cost and Performance: Implications for Public and industry Policies*. Center for transportation Studies, University of British Columbia, Canada.

Gillen, D.W., T.H. Oum and M.W. Tretheway (1990) Airline cost structure and policy implications. *Journal of Transport Economics and Policy* 24, 9-34.

Gronau, R. (1986) Home production - a survey. In O. Ashenfelter and R. Layard, eds., *Handbook of Labor Economics* 1, North Holland, 273 - 304.

Harmatuck, D.J. (1981) A motor carrier joint cost function. *Journal of Transport Economics and Policy*, 21 135-153.

Harmatuck, D.J. (1985) Short run motor carrier cost function for five large common carriers. *Logistics and Transportation Review* 21, 217-237.

Harmatuck, D.J., (1991) Economies of scale and scope in the motor carrier industry. *Journal of Transport Economics and Policy* 25, 135-151.

Hausman, J. (1981) Exact consumer's surplus and deadweight loss. *American Economic Review* 71, 662-676.

Hicks, J. R. (1956) A Revision of Demand Theory, Oxford. Oxford University Press.

Hotelling, H. (1938) The general welfare in relation to problems of taxation and of railway and utility rates. *Econometrica* 6, 242-269,

Jacobsen, S.E. (1979) On the equivalence of input and output market Marshallian surplus measures. *American Economic Review* 69, 423-428.

Jansson, J.O. (1979) Marginal cost pricing of scheduled transport services. Journal of Transport Economics and Policy 13, 268-294.

Jara-Díaz, S.R. (1982a) The estimation of transport cost functions: a methodological review. *Transport Reviews* 2, 257-278.

Jara-Díaz, S.R. (1982b) Transportation product, transportation function and cost functions. *Transportation Science* 16, 522-539.

Jara-Díaz, S.R. (1986) On the relation between users' benefits and the economic effects of transportation activities. *Journal of Regional Science* 26, 379-391.

Jara-Díaz, S.R. (1990). Consumer's surplus and the value of travel time savings. *Transportation Research* 24B, 73-77.

Jara-Díaz, S.R. (1991) Income and taste in mode choice models: are they surrogates? *Transportation Research* 25B, 341 - 350.

Jara-Díaz, S.R. (1998) Time and Income in travel choice: towards a microeconomic activity-based theoretical framework. In *Theoretical Foundations of Travel Choice Models*, Tommy Gärling, Thomas Laitila and Kerstin Westin, eds. Elsevier, Oxford, 51-73.

Jara-Díaz, S.R. (2000) Transport production and the analysis of industry structure. In *Analytical Transport Economics, an international perspective*, Jacob Polak and Arnold Heertje, eds. Elgar: Cheltenham, UK, 27-50.

Jara-Díaz, S.R. (2003) On the Goods-Activities Technical Relations in the Time Allocation Theory. *Transportation* 30, 245-260.

Jara-Díaz, S.R. and T. Friesz(1982) Measuring the benefits derived from a transportation investment. *Transportation Research 16B*, 57-77.

Jara-Díaz, S.R. and M. Farah (1987) Transport demand and users' benefits with fixed income: the goods/leisure trade off revisited. *Transportation Research 21B*, 165-170.

Jara-Díaz, S.R. and J. de D. Ortúzar (1989) Introducing the expenditure rate in the estimation of mode choice models. *Journal of Transport Economics and Policy* 23, 293 - 308.

Jara-Díaz, S.R. and J. Videla (1989) Detection of income effect in mode choice: theory and application. *Transportation Research* 23B, 393 - 400.

Jara-Díaz, S.R. and J. Videla (1990). Welfare implications of the omission of income effect in mode choice models. *Journal of Transport Economics and Policy* 24, 83-93.

Jara-Díaz, S.R., P. Donoso and J. Araneda (1991) Best partial flow aggregation in transportation cost functions. *Transportation Research 25B*, 329-339.

Jara-Díaz, S.R., P. Donoso and J. Araneda (1992) Estimation of marginal transport costs using the flow aggregation function approach. *Journal of Transport Economics and Policy* 26, 35-48.

Jara-Díaz, S.R. and C. Cortés (1996) On the calculation of scale economies from transport cost functions. *Journal of Transport Economics and Policy* 30, 157-170.

Jara-Díaz, S.R., T. Gálvez and C. Vergara (2000) Social Valuation of road accident reductions using subjective perceptions. *Journal of Transport Economics and Policy* 34(2), 215-232.

Jara-Díaz, S.R., C. Cortés and F. Ponce (2001). Number of points served and economies of spatial scope in transport cost functions. *Journal of Transport Economics and Policy* 35(2), 327-341.

Jara-Díaz, S.R. and L. Basso (2003) Transport cost functions, network expansion and economies of scope. *Transportation Research* 39E, 269-286.

Jara-Díaz, S.R. and A. Guevara (2003). Behind the subjective value of travel time savings: the perception of work, leisure and travel from a joint mode choice - activity model. *Journal of Transport Economics and Policy* 37, 29-46.

Jara-Díaz, S.R., C. Vergara and T. Gálvez (2006) A methodology to calculate social values for air pollution using discrete choice models. *Transport Reviews* 26, 435-449.

Johnson, B. (1966) Travel time and the price of leisure. *Western Economic Journal*, Spring, 135 - 145.

Keaton, M.H. (1990) Economies of density and service levels on U.S. Railroads: an experimental analysis, *Logistics and Transportation Review* 26, 211-227.

Keeler, J. and J.P. Formby (1994) Cost economies and consolidation in the U.S. airline industry, *International Journal of Transport Economics* 21, 21-45.

Kim, M. (1987) Multilateral relative efficiency levels in regional Canadian trucking. *Logistics and Transportation Review* 23, 155-173.

Kirby, M.G. (1986) Airline Economies of 'Scale' and the Australian Domestic Air Transport Policy. *Journal of Transport Economics and Policy* 20(3), 339-352.

Koshal, R.K. and M. Koshal (1989) Economies of scale of state road transport industry in India. *International Journal of Transport Economics* 16, 165-173.

Kumbhakar, S.C (1992) Allocative Distortions, Technical Progress and Input Demand in U.S. Airlines: 1970:1984. *International Economic Review* 33(3), 723-737

Lancaster, K. (1966) A new approach to consumer theory. *Journal of Political Economy* 74, 132 - 157.

Liu, Z. and Lynk, E.L. (1999) Evidence on Market Structure of the Deregulated US Airline Industry, *Applied Economics 31*, 1083-1092.

Malinvaud, E. (1969) Lecons de Théorie Microéconomique. Dunod, Paris.

Marshall, A. (1920) Principles of Economics, 8th ed. Macmillan, London.

McFadden, D. (1981) Econometric models of probabilistic choice. In: *Structural Analysis of Discrete Data with Econometric Applications*, C. Manski and D. McFadden, eds. MIT Press, Cambridge, MA.

Meyer, J.R., J.F. Kain and M. Wohl (1965) The Urban Transportation Problem, Harvard U. Press, Mass.

Michael, R, and G. Becker (1973) On the new theory of consumer behavior. *Swedish Journal of Economics* 75, 378 - 396.

Mishan, E. J. (1976) Cost-Benefit Analysis. Praeger, New York.

Mohring, H. (1976) Transportation Economics. Ballinger, Cambridge.

Morey, E. R. (1984) Consumer surplus. *American Economic Review* 74, 163-173.

Neuberger, H.L.L (1971) User benefits in the evaluation of transport and land use plans. *Journal of Transport Economic and Policy* 6, 52-75.

Oort, C. (1969) The evaluation of travelling time. *Journal of Transport Economics and Policy*, September, 279 - 286.

Ortúzar, J. de D. and González, R. M. (2002) Inter-island travel demand response with discrete choice models - Functional form, forecasts, and elasticities. *Journal of Transport Economics and Policy* 36, 115-138.

Oum, T.H. and Zhang, Y. (1991) Utilisation of Quasi-Fixed Inputs and estimation of Cost

Functions. *Journal of Transports Economics and Policy* 25, 121-134.

Oum, T.H. and Zhang, Y. (1997) A Note on Scale Economies in Transport. *Journal of Transport Economics and Policy* 31, 309-315.

Oum, T.H., Park, J-H. and Zhang, A. (2000) Globalization and Strategic Alliances: the Case of the Airline Industry. Pergamon, Elsevier Science

Oum, T.O and W.G. Waters II (1996) A survey of recent developments in transportation cost function research. *Logistics and Transportation Review* 32, 423-463.

Panzar, J.C and R.D Willig (1977) Economies of scale in multioutput production. *Quarterly journal of Economics 91*, August: 481-493.

Pearce, D.W. and C.A. Nash (1981) A Text in Cost-Benefit Analysis. Macmillan, London.

Pollak R. and M. Wachter (1975) The relevance of the household production function and its implications for the allocation of time. *Journal of Political Economy* 83(2), 255-277.

Sasaki, K. (1982) Travel demand and the evaluation of transportation system change: a reconsideration of the random utility approach. *Environment and Planning A*14, 169-182.

Small, K. (1982) Scheduling of consumer activities: Work trips. *American Economic Review* 72, 467-479.

Small, K.A., and H. S. Rosen (1981) Applied welfare economics with discrete choice models. *Econometrica* 49, 105-129.

Spady, R. and A.F. Friedlaender (1978) Hedonic cost functions for the regulated trucking industry. *Bell Journal of Economics* 9, 159-179.

Tauchen, H., F.D. Fravel and G. Gilbert (1983) Cost structure in the intercity bus industry. *Journal of Transport Economics and Policy* 17, 25-47.

Thomson, J. M. (1974) Modern Transport Economics. Penguin Books, Harmondsworth.

Train, K. and D. McFadden (1978) The goods / leisure trade-off and disaggregate work trip mode choice models. *Transportation Research* 12, 349 - 353.

Truong, P. and D. Hensher (1985) Measurement of travel time values and opportunity cost from a discrete - choice model. *The Economic Journal* 95, 438 - 451.

Varian, H.R. (1978) Microeconomic Analysis. Norton, New York.

Viton, P. (1985) On the interpretation of income variables in discrete choice models. *Economic Letters* 17, 203 - 206.

Wang Chiang, S.J. and A.F. Friedlaender (1984) Output aggregation, network effects, and the measurement of trucking technology. *Review of Economics and Statistics* 66, 267-276.

Wilson, A.G. (1967) A statistical theory of spatial distribution models. *Transportation Research* 1, 253-269.

Williams, H.C.W.L. (1976) Travel demand models, duality relations and user benefit analysis. *Journal of Regional Science* 16, 147-166.

Williams, H.C.W.L. (1977) On the formation of travel demand models - and economic evaluation measures of user benefit. *Environment and Planning A* 9, 285 344.

Willig, R., (1976) Consumer's surplus without apology. *American Economic Review* 66, 589-597.

Windle, R.J. (1991) The world's airlines. *Journal of Transport Economics and Policy* 25, 31-49.

Xu, K., C. Windle. C. Grimm and T. Corsi (1994) Re-evaluating Returns to Scale in Transport. *Journal of Transport Economics and Policy*, September, 275-286.

Ying, J.S. (1990) The inefficiency of regulating a competitive industry: productivity gains in trucking following reform. *Review of Economics and Statistics* 72, 191-201.

Ying, J.S. (1992) On calculating cost elasticities. *Logistics and Transportation Review* 28, 231-235.

Ying, J.S. and T.E. Keeler (1991) Pricing in a deregulated environment: the motor carrier experience. *Rand Journal of Economics* 22, 264-273.

Index

O

o-d structure, 12, 13, 17, 23, 28, 29, 31, 32
Oort, C., 64, 66, 67, 68, 134
operating rules, 11, 12, 13, 15, 19, 26, 47
operators, 7, 8, 112, 113, 115, 116, 117, 118, 119, 120, 125
optimal prices, 8, 111, 112, 113, 114, 115, 116, 118, 120, 121, 127, 128, 129
Ortúzar, J.deD., 3, 57, 62, 133, 134
Oum, T.H., 36, 41, 44, 132, 134

P

Panzar, J.C., 19, 21, 131, 134
Park, J-H., 44, 134
passengers-kilometers, 36, 37, 39, 46, 48
patronage, 111, 112, 115, 123, 127, 128, 129
Pearce, D.W., 107, 134
personal/household income , 3, 52, 81, 82
points served, 8, 36, 41, 42, 133
Pollak, R., 134
Ponce, F., 43, 133
possibility frontier, 16, 17, 19, 26
private transport, 9, 36, 51, 53, 62, 78, 87, 88, 117, 118, 119, 120, 126, 128
product, 7, 9, 11, 12, 13, 15, 20, 22, 23, 25, 30, 31, 32, 40, 41, 42, 43, 44, 47, 48, 102, 106, 111, 125, 132
profit, 105, 112, 121, 125, 127, 128, 129
public transport, 9, 111, 118, 119, 120, 127, 131

Q

qualitative changes , 98

R

returns to density, 41, 44, 48
returns to scale, 19, 41, 114, 131
revenue, 36, 112, 113, 121, 122, 125
Rich, D.P., 41, 131
right-of-way, 19, 24, 27
Roberts, M., 61, 131
Rosen, H.S., 98, 134
route structure, 8, 12, 13, 14, 17, 18, 19, 26, 27, 28, 29, 30, 37, 40, 42, 46, 47
rule-of-the-half, 81, 83, 85, 87, 88, 110

S

Sasaki, K., 89, 98, 134
second best pricing, 114, 126
sensitivity to price, 125, 127
service structure, 12, 13, 14, 17, 23, 27, 47

Shephard's Lemma, 21, 33
Slutsky, 94, 97, 100, 101, 110
Small, K., 67, 69, 98, 134
social price of time, 106, 108, 109
social utility, 107, 108
social utility of money, 108
social welfare, 9, 107
socio-economic, 53, 55, 62, 100, 110
Spady, R., 33, 35, 36, 134
Spiller, P.T., 41, 131
subadditivity, 22, 33, 42
subjective value, 55, 59, 61, 64, 78, 79, 99, 100, 107, 108, 109, 128, 133
  of travel time savings, 55, 59, 61, 62, 64, 68, 106, 107, 109, 133
Swanson, J.A., 41, 131

T

Tauchen, H., 36, 134
taylor expansion, 32, 56, 60, 86, 100
technology, 11
terminal operations, 25, 28
Thistle, P.D., 132
Thomson, J.M., 87, 134
time constraint, 63, 67, 70, 71, 72, 73, 78, 79
Train, K., 57, 63, 70, 134
transformation function, 11, 14, 15, 17, 19, 66, 70, 71, 79
transport firms, 3, 8, 11, 12, 13, 15, 20, 26, 31, 32, 111, 114, 121
transport output, 3, 8, 11, 12, 18, 19, 23, 31, 32, 34, 37, 47, 133
transport production, 3, 8, 11, 12, 18, 19, 23, 34, 37, 47, 133
travel choice, 52, 54, 55, 57, 76, 77, 78, 109, 131, 133
travel time, 15, 47, 51, 52, 55, 57, 59, 60, 61, 62, 64, 66, 67, 69, 70, 72, 77, 79, 99, 106, 107, 109, 110, 118, 128, 131, 132, 133, 135
Tretheway, M.W., 41, 131, 132
truncated conditional indirect utility, 54, 55, 59, 60
Truong, P., 62, 70, 135

U

utility function, 52, 53, 54, 55, 56, 58, 62, 63, 64, 69, 75, 78, 88, 91, 99

V

value of time , 8, 51, 59, 61, 63, 64, 65, 66, 67, 68, 70, 71, 73, 76, 77, 79, 109, 116, 132
variable network size, 42, 131
Varian, H.R., 91, 135